QUILOMBOLA!

Series Editor

LÉONORA MIANO

Quilombola is a Brazilian word for the inhabitant of a maroon, or 'runaway-slave' community. The choice of this appellation is a tribute to those who, throughout human history, have stood up against oppression. However, there is more in this reference: it speaks both about freedom regained and about all the creative gestures that stemmed from that conquest. For those who had broken their chains, the *quilombo* was a place of reappropriation and reinvention of oneself.

It is by inviting writers and readers to practice *marronnage*—'running away from slavery'—of thought, to shift their way of thinking, that the series **Quilombola!** stands out. This list of books is a space from which resonate insubordinate, inventive, provocative and unexpected voices. Whether artists, activists or intellectuals, the authors of **Quilombola!** bring a sensitive reflection on the world and forge new paths. Although focusing on sub-Saharan African and French-speaking Afropean expressions, we welcome minority points of view from other places too.

The series aims at making itself accessible to a large readership in order to promote a wider circulation of thought. It is on this condition that it will come to meaningful fruition.

Afropea

A Post-Western and Post-Racist Utopia

LÉONORA MIANO

TRANSLATED BY
GILA WALKER

LONDON NEW YORK CALCUTTA

PAP
TAGORE

This work is published with the support of the
Publication Assistance Programmes of the Institut français

Seagull Books, 2024

Originally published in French as Léonora Miano,
Afropea: *Utopie post-occidentale et post-raciste*
© Éditions Grasset & Fasquelle, Paris, 2020

First published in English translation by Seagull Books, 2024

English translation © Gila Walker, 2024

ISBN 978 1 8030 9 342 0

British Library Cataloguing-in-Publication Data
A catalogue record for this book is available from the British Library

Typeset by Seagull Books, Calcutta, India
Printed and bound by WordsWorth India, New Delhi, India

I would say that it is a specific culture, at a precise period in its evolution, with its worldview and its limits, with its tales and its myths, that was used to dominate and despoil others by threatening them with a hell of its own imagination. It is therefore by other cultures that this ransacking can and must be corrected.

WEREWERE LIKING

The West is not in the West. It is a project, not a place.

ÉDOUARD GLISSANT

For this is your home, my friend, do not be driven from it.

JAMES BALDWIN

CONTENTS

Preamble

As a preamble, indicate the following: I am not an Afropean. There were times I let people say I was, out of lassitude rather than laziness. You cannot be continually providing instruction during interviews with interlocutors who show little desire to actually know how things stand. For most people in metropolitan France, the prefix Afro can only refer to an elsewhere, to an outside France that is more essential than original. This is what justifies classifying in the category of Afropean any individual of sub-Saharan descent living in the country. Especially if the choice of this space occurred some time ago. Even more if the person concerned seems to be well versed in social codes. In this case, she will be allowed to define herself as a European coming from that beyond alter-world that is Africa in the eyes of many. A European *avec des origines*, literally 'with origins', an idiotic expression used in France to designate any de facto foreignness. In a country where the expression *issu de l'immigration*, 'originating from immigration', seems to have acquired an ontological character, this misconception is hardly surprising. European France's imaginary vigorously resists renewal and has difficulty digesting the most blatant realities.

So here is the definition: an Afropean is a person of sub-Saharan descent born and raised in Europe. Individuals with this profile were the ones who promoted this ethnicity, claimed it as their own and aspired to embody it. The people concerned are first and foremost repositories of a European experience. It is in Europe that they spent their formative years, those of childhood and adolescence, whose importance for structuring personality is well known. Afropeans are often the children, grandchildren or great-grandchildren of sub-Saharan immigrants. Unlike their forebears, they have always lived as a minority, in a space loath to see itself in them.

I, on the other hand, was fortunate to have been born and raised in sub-Saharan Africa where my aspirations were never derailed by the colour of my skin. I did not suffer from a lack of representation and I was pleased to live in France precisely because I was not *at home*, in the usual sense of the expression. Being a foreigner is not necessarily painful. The singularity of my profile, its utterly marginal character, wherever I am, always puts me in this situation. I do not see it as a problem. The different worlds that constitute me enable me to understand them all without the reverse being possible, and to choose most of my affiliations. The only one that is visceral is also the one that is most often denied me, for I am told that I am not an authentic sub-Saharan. They are wrong, but I do not correct them. I know what disturbs them, the way a profile such as mine confronts sub-Saharans with the colonial past, and hence with the loss of a part of themselves. I am the fruit of uncommon backgrounds. Unlike me, both my parents came to know France when they were young, having spent time there with their families. Still today my mother has enchanting memories of her arrival in Paris a few days before Christmas, when Place de la Concorde was aglow with lights. She was ten years old. In the Cirque d'Hiver district where the family lived, near metro Filles-du-Calvaire, people would lean out of their windows to watch my grandmother escorting her girls to school.

As a result, the distance from French society was relative since neither the language nor the cultural references were alien to me. My foreignness gave me the unfettered freedom to finish forging my character. It granted me the precious right to make mistakes, to live through experiences in the comfort of an anonymity that I would not have had in Cameroon. The hardships led me to face myself and discover unsuspected resources within. Being an immigrant was not always a picnic, but it brought me so much. And it greatly helped with the exposure from which I benefitted quite quickly as an author. In literary circles, my 'selling point', to use marketing jargon, resides in my sub-Saharan identity. People could not care less about my French citizenship. The latter only acquires a semblance of value when I am abroad, invited by the French cultural services, eager to show that France is open to the world. Nowadays this is indispensable for it to maintain its place. France is therefore more willing to embrace people originating from its former colonies than to associate with its margins. The most high-profile Black writers in France are sub-Saharan or Haitian, seldom Afropean.

Consequently, my relationship with France differs considerably from the kind Afropeans have with their country. They tend to be extremely touchy about things that bother me only mildly. For instance, I do not see a representation of sub-Saharan figures in the group parading in Dunkirk's Night of the Blacks carnival. Nothing in those crassly dressed-up characters strikes me as having anything at all to do with me and mine. All I see are typical French peculiarities demonstrating once again how impossible it is to uncover and assume the presence of the other within oneself, to acknowledge one's intimacy with the other, except by resorting to caricature. In doing so, nothing can be said about the other. It does not in fact concern the other. The costume's ugliness speaks of distress and turmoil, which only elicits deep empathy from me for those who engage in such a process. If they were to parade through some sub-Saharan environment, they would be jeered and heckled emphatically. No one would think of protesting against an offence. They would be seen as Whites doing their White things; after all, sub-Saharans have had enough experience with them to know that they have a screw loose.

The Afropean reaction to this is very different, and understandably so. They live in a racialized environment, marked by inequality in representation, as in all other areas of social life. Great pains are taken to make sure that the projected image of Afro-descendants is never of the kind that would instil a sense of power in them, or even, simply, of being at ease with who they are. Ridicule and degradation are always there, lurking in the shadows, ready to rear their heads at the proper time. Incompetent or unremarkable people will sometimes be put in the spotlight so as to silence complaints about policies of equitable representation. Their failure will then serve as a pretext for refusing inclusion. When that is not the case, the zeal with which the chosen ones will bend over backwards to conform to the clichés of the system will be rewarded with cheers and promotions. It is at this price that they will earn the right to occupy the place of the court jester, without being permitted to reveal that the king is naked. The terms of this tacit agreement are clear. Those who have ratified it will occasionally adopt tones of protest. They will, however, avoid divisive subjects, those that are polarizing in France. They will formulate vehement critiques of sub-Saharan autocrats, at no cost to anyone.

The Afro presence, which is still too disruptive within French society, must be entertaining above all, no matter how this goal is achieved. Without even speaking of the racist practice of blackface evidenced by the Dunkirk masquerading, it is an act of aggression when members of the dominant ethnic group arrogate the right to put on makeup to look like those whom they do not even want to see. The opposite would not have the same impact and would not occur to anyone. Confronted with such disguises, sub-Saharans and Afropeans do not react the same way, as they are the product of different realities. Self-perception, the way we look at ourselves, depends to a great extent on what we receive from society and from our own community. In sub-Saharan Africa, notwithstanding the upheavals of history and the damage to the psyche, one is first and foremost a person. In Europe, when you are of sub-Saharan descent, you are a foreigner belonging to a group deprived of power, which can be exposed to all kinds of caricatures and denials. And you are enjoined to embrace your individuality only to see yourself invited, by the same injunction, to dissociate yourself from your community. If necessary, you will have to contribute to its debasement.

The erasure of the Afropean presence leads some to consider the mere fact of people from the majority group doing their hair or dressing in sub-Saharan style as an act of cultural appropriation. In Africa, this would not bother anyone. They would see it rather as a celebration of their culture and would be flattered. Sub-Saharans saw nothing shocking in Bo Derek's braids in Blake Edwards' 1979 movie *10*. We wore exactly the same braids and they looked good on her, so it was considered a fitting tribute. It was not even remotely related to dispossessing artists of their creation to make money. We would continue to wear our hair like that; nothing had been stolen from us. Today the image of Bo Derek has become a symbol of cultural appropriation and identity plundering, as if cultures could be transmitted by capillary pathways.

I wondered about how other cultures react when their adornments and clothing styles are adopted by foreigners, so I brought up the question during my trips to India and Japan. In both countries, the reaction was identical to that of sub-Saharans living on the continent. Things are different in Western societies where minorities tolerate such things less and less. Because they are not seen or heard. Because wearing their hair or dressing in exactly the same way is negatively perceived as evidencing poor assimilation. Because the members of the majority group adopt these costumes only sporadically, and often for fun or even in jest. And because they are ostracized due to their sub-Saharan origin, Afropeans tend to turn a headscarf or a wrap into an emblem of cultures that they often hardly know. The pain, frustration and impotence have them grasping at the most superficial attributes of their ancestral culture. They find themselves defending a territory that they feel is threatened even before it is established.

On the other hand, Afropean protests died down when the movie *Black Panther* (2018) traded in sub-Saharan styles, mixing them as it saw fit, to compose a cinematographic Africa. In such a case, sub-Saharan descent is considered license to do whatever one pleases. After all, the whole of Africa is the property of all Blacks. Everybody knows that. Never mind about those among the peoples of the continent who might be tempted to see things otherwise. Solidarity between sub-Saharans and Afro-descendants will not develop organically. It is not self-evident. A great many sub-Saharans are in no way connected to the populations that originated from transoceanic deportations. They have no obligation to automatically include them in their plans. It is important to keep this in mind, even if it is distressing. Furthermore, what kind of respect can people expect when they behave in the same way as their oppressor? When they arrogate the right to project their fantasies on human groups solely because they have the same complexion?

The sub-Saharan space chosen to create Wakanda, the fictional kingdom where the story of *Black Panther* is set, is alien to Afro-descendants in Brazil, the United States, France and all the other countries where people delighted in standing, arms crossed over their chests, reciting the mantra, 'Wakanda forever'. Given that being Black is first and foremost a political condition resulting from Western domination, it could not concern the inhabitants of Wakanda who prided themselves on never having lived under a colonial yoke. The story of *Black Panther* thus took place in a kingdom that could not have spawned a Black hero. There were no Blacks in Wakanda. Perhaps no Africans either. This fact seems to have escaped the attention of the most informed commentators. They all see the world solely through the lens of the imperialist and racist conceptions that they lambast from morning to night.

It is in the entertainment industry that the question of cultural appropriation is most strongly posed at the moment, leading to polemics on the part of those who make as if they do not understand. It is not a matter of French people belonging to minority groups claiming that human experience cannot be understood or embodied by all, even though some think this is so. The question, to my mind, is not philosophical, and not primarily an issue of identity. It is political and economic.[1] It is a matter of knowing who has the right to express themselves and occupy the space; who has the right to get rich and see their creations celebrated. As long as an Afro-descendant actor cannot play the part of General de Gaulle on screen, Gérard Depardieu in the role of Alexandre Dumas will necessarily be perceived as offensive. It is impossible to advocate universalism and only ever give it Caucasian features.

Here is another example of the difference in standpoint between sub-Saharans and Afropeans. For the latter, the tribute

---

1 Witness Disney's attempt to patent the Swahili expression *hakuna matata*.

paid to colonial soldiers is of capital importance. The memory of sub-Saharans who enlisted in conflicts on the side of France legitimates the presence of their descendants on French soil. They are among the references on which hinges the right to be in France and call oneself French. Their remains are sometimes buried in French soil, the country for which they gave their lives. Paying tribute to them is a way of recognizing those who regard them as immediate ancestors, even if it is only a symbolic and not necessarily biological kinship. But if France owes everything to the sub-Saharans that served it, voluntarily or by force, Africa, on the other hand, owes them nothing. In fact, just the opposite.

The Afropean will make a hero of a person that the sub-Saharan will perceive at best as the victim of manipulation, at worst as a traitor who committed unpardonable crimes. Either way, for a sub-Saharan, it is impossible to celebrate the pathway these colonial soldiers chose. They did not only fight France's European enemies. They were also used against colonized populations in Asia and Africa. In many cases, they were zealous agents, mercenaries of colonial politics. In sub-Saharan Africa, some took power after independence and excelled at totalitarianism, with the fervent backing of the former colonizer. Afropeans, on the other hand, despite their attachment to the African continent, do not reject the figure of colonial soldier. This figure stands as an indispensable component of their memory, identity and heritage that entitles them to claim their place in France.

From these examples of the way in which consciousness of identity is articulated according to affiliation, we can see how experience influences the positions taken and one's being-in-the-world itself. Acquiring French citizenship has no effect on this reality. No amount of time spent abroad suffices to remove what Africa gives to its children. So from where does my interest in Afropea stem and why have I felt the need to include it in some of my writings? The answer is simple: I gave birth to a girl in France. My daughter is now a young woman who is so French that the sub-Saharan in me cannot help but see her as exotic at times. Like many parents who came from the African continent, I can testify to the way in which we sometimes feel that our children escape us without knowing for sure that loving arms will be there to catch them in their flight. Maybe this is the lot of all parents.

In France, we are ungrounded, and deprived of our family or community most of the time. Our names mean nothing. Our genealogies are abolished there. This is felt most intensely when, for a variety of reasons, living in France coincides with downward mobility. This was the case for many of us from the middle class who came from Central Africa in the early 1990s when our families were hit hard by the depreciation of the CFA franc. The collapse was brutal at times and the children who had been sent abroad had to endure previously unthinkable living conditions. Some did not get over it. The well-off, or those who are purported to be, have a community to bring it their support. They are the ones to whom people turn for help and who must expect nothing in return. People of their caste will keep away from them because they fear that misfortune is contagious, and because times have changed and they are all trying to hide their own hardships. Having experienced both a loss of status, and a blunting of one's individuality due to racialization, sub-Saharans from a once-privileged class will not for that matter dissolve into the Afropean population. Their difference creates a distance complicating recognition. They will be part of a minority within the minority, as their presence will be too singular to be fully adopted. On this subject, many anecdotes come to mind. I will mention only one and a half.

In the mid-90s, when I, like many others, was living hand-to-mouth, working seven days a week and never really making ends meet, I would occasionally bring my daughter with me to the place where I was employed. This would usually happen on Saturday or Sunday, for obvious reasons. The first time, she had just turned three, and we had to travel across Paris from east to west early in the morning. Astonished looks greeted us, followed by whispering. Discreetly they came to observe the phenomenon: this little girl in the office, quietly drawing while I went about my business. The observers were of sub-Saharan or Maghrebi descent, which has its importance here. In the past as in the present, people from colonized countries are overrepresented when jobs are both unappealing and low-paying. Why were they looking at us incredulously? Why were they whispering? It turned out that the little one was Black and did not coincide with the perception they had of me.

It seemed so abnormal to them that one young woman whose parents were Guinean could not keep herself from asking and exclaiming in a single breath, 'That's your daughter? But . . . she's not mixed race!' My language, my attitude and who knows what else made them associate me with Whiteness. I was not the kind of woman they would imagine copulating with Blacks. I was not Black in the sense that it was understood in the poor neighbourhoods on the city's outskirts, and probably never would be. Many years later, in secondary school, my daughter would be rejected by other French people of sub-Saharan descent. 'You're not a real Black,' they would throw in her face. My social condition did not matter, neither did the fact that I had gone through hardships that many were spared because I had not yet acquired French nationality. I was different: neither the ordinary girl from the boondocks (strong accent, questionable syntax and limited vocabulary), nor a sharp, shrill girl from the projects; neither an educated Negropolitan in search of a colour-neutral tomorrow, nor a trendy Afropolitan loudly conjuring Africa with colourful clothing. And definitely not a *Noirabe*, the term used to designate a Black person influenced by Maghrebi culture. They simply did not know in what category to put me. Some of this foreignness was passed on to my daughter. I did not put much effort into making it easier for people to get a handle on me, having very early decided not to try to please or be understood by everyone.

Some things were surely easier for me than they must have been for others, because I was raising a girl and because I had received enough of a Westernized education to understand French society and provide my little princess with proper guidance. This was the meagre advantage that my social background gave me. A moneyless bourgeoise still retains her cultural capital. Mine was often of great assistance. Nevertheless, the most Europeanized sub-Saharan is not and will never be a European, no matter what. This too I am in a position to affirm. Identification with us by the French who share our complexion remains frustrated, even after years of living in the country. Our life experience is only partly the same as theirs. We *represent*, as they say, only when it is a matter of the global Blackness that transcends nationalities and speaks of a common wound. In a country where the local Blackness has yet to define its contours or discourses, embodying a global condition still involves speaking only to a minority within the minority: intellectuals and artists, generally Afro-Americanized. We represent the original continent, to be sure. But for historical reasons, it is seen, in France, as a big Senegal or a giant Mali. In this respect too, no one knows where to situate you, and sub-Saharan authenticity is once again contested. Whence the questions that the French of European descent ask: 'Why did you choose the name Léonora?' 'Because it's my name.' The thing is inconceivable. You are expected to be called Fatou, Salimata, Djeneba, or any other name that does not remind them that sub-Saharans were colonized, their identities altered.

You could not have had a mother who was an English teacher and sang Mozart's lullaby to her girls, taught them 'It's a Long Way to Tipperary', and read 'The Canterville Ghost' to them. You could not have had a father who was a pharmacist, a lover of jazz, music hall and Westerns. You could not have, during that same childhood, played jakasi and mbang, danced unrestrained to Makossa, hunted grasshoppers before frying them in a pan, learnt how to grind condiments with a stone, and to kill, gut and pluck a chicken for dinner. You cannot have all these worlds within you, it is confusing in the end. France pretends to delight in mixtures, but there is always something suspicious about the result. Leaving aside these aspects, the time spent in France and the attachment to this country can do nothing to counter the rumblings of the Africa that inhabits us and often claims its due. The land calls you and you must heed the call. That is the way it is: citizenship and identity do not always become perfect synonyms. We are first the fruit of a personal history. I come from an era and a background in which ending up in France was a bit like having failed your life. The sub-Saharan bourgeoisie has its contradictions, which are not really as contradictory as they might seem at first glance. They would envy some of your advantages but pity you nonetheless. It was necessary to be able to go to France easily, own property there, why not, but life, real life, was lived at home. In a country that knows your name. A country where strangers you met on the street could name your ancestors just by looking at you. A country where instead of asking, 'What's your name?' people say, 'Whose child are you?' Those days and those worlds are gone.

Be that as it may, it is the mother in me who, intent on preparing my daughter's future in this place that is *her home* but that would soon refuse to embrace her, conceived of the work on Afropea as a matter of urgency. It was for my daughter's sake that I made up my mind to apply for French citizenship. I was beginning to earn some money from my books and wanted to introduce her to the world. Born French, haunted as a child by the fear of seeing me deported, she would have watched me being subjected at airports to differential, often degrading treatments. I refused this.

Since Cameroon did not accept dual nationalities, it seemed risky to impose on her an affiliation that might not suit her. I do not regret this sacrifice. She and I have always known that one was European, the other sub-Saharan. We speak the same language. Having learnt only French from my parents, it was impossible for me to transmit Duala to her, a language I studied on my own in an effort to gain access to the world that grownups were concealing from me. So here is how it is: I think in French most of the time, I feel in Duala, I dream in three languages at least, as English has always been part of my life. I started learning it at the age of two in a private preschool in Duala, at the time when Cameroon considered it imperative that young people have a command of its two official languages: French and English.

In 2007, France chose to entrust its destiny to Nicolas Sarkozy, which opened the floodgates to expressions of racism that had been more inhibited until then. It became necessary to provide the country with the instruments that would enable it to grasp this unthought Afropean presence. I wrote a few texts, which is what I know how to do. France being a country of literature, that is, a country that sees itself and presents itself to the world through literary texts, it was time to start at least tackling the job. Anything that does not appear in French literature does not exist for the country. And the fact is, there is no Afropean corpus. I felt it was my duty to reveal these other faces of France, to make their voices heard. Of course, it was important to name those concerned. This was the precondition not only of formalizing their existence but also of underscoring the particularities of the Afro-descendant experiences on European soil. I did not wish to subscribe to racial terminology. Although its political value is attested, it remains powerless to say what humans are and to help people identify with them. Bringing into play Afropea was of the essence, even though the concept is still not widely used. No doubt this is due to what it evokes, to its project for society, to the aspirations it pursues, to the way in which it breaks down what were thought to be load-bearing walls. This is what I would like to explore in these pages: say why Afropea seems to me to be a wellspring from which we can draw in order to renew imaginaries and forge new relational modalities.

In this essay—whose subjectivity, intuitiveness and hybridity I fully acknowledge—Afropea embodies the populations in the Northern hemisphere that were brutalized first by conqueror-Europe starting in the late fifteenth century, and then by what has been called the West. Which is another way of designating capitalism and its violence. The venality inherent to Westernity is what engendered the concept of race as we know it today. We owe the racialization of bodies and imaginaries to Westernity's domination. The West is no longer limited to the human groups with roots in Western Europe, even though they were at the origin of this system and remain its main beneficiaries. The West is also the way the spirit that gave rise to this phenomenon of racialization, which spread across the planet under colonial influence, acclimatized so as to transform views of the world and of the self in the world.

The ancient Chinese who invented the compass, gunpowder and the rudder did not use these to conquer territories and populations beyond their continent of origin, to impose their beliefs, their language or their writing, and reduce them to slavery. Their imperialism and violence did not give rise to planetary ambitions. This was not because they lacked knowledge of the world. China and Africa have been in contact for much longer than is typically said. The study of their relations across the Indian Ocean reveals a history that dates back to the ninth century, which corresponds in Europe to the High Middle Ages.[2] The transoceanic deportations of sub-Saharans—that concern the Indian Ocean—and the colonial occupation of Africa did not occur to the Chinese of yesteryear. Those who in the more recent past stood by the side of the young sub-Saharan states, like Modibo Keita's socialist Mali, did not have colonial ambitions either.

The China of today, which has steadfastly hatched its revenge against the unequal treaties,[3] which is reinventing the Silk Road to establish its hegemony over the world, which is installing military bases in Africa, which is extending its reach to the field of cultural influence, which is feverishly and ferociously engaged in capitalist competition, this China is Westernized. The Westernization, which is expressed in the means and in the acts, serves in this case to return blows, to be rid of protracted humiliations, to beat the other at their

2 François Bart, 'Chine et Afrique, une longue histoire, une nouvelle donne géographique' [China and Africa, a long history, a new geographic situation], *Les Cahiers d'Outre-Mer* 253–54 (2011): 193–208.

3 In the nineteenth century, the opium wars ended with the signing of a series of treaties that divided China into eight zones and assigned them to Western powers (United Kingdom of Great Britain and Northern Ireland, France, United Kingdoms of Sweden and Norway, United States of America, Russia, Portugal, and the Germanic Confederation). These treaties considerably limited China's sovereignty and unconditionally opened the country up to foreign appetites.

own game. China invests more in Europe than it does in Africa where its presence alarms the former colonizers, ever ready to accept Chinese capital investments while looking askance at the fact that sub-Saharans do the same. China will take its revenge first on European soil, which is only logical. Other illustrations would serve to demonstrate the reshaping of mental architecture by Westernity in all the spaces on which it was imposed.

I will use the terms Europe and France almost interchangeably. Having taken a name that transcends national borders, Afropea is lodged for the time being in the nations of which it is a native and a citizen. If pan-Africanism is as yet a fiction, European federalism is not a reality either. This being the case, and also because I know it the best, the French context will be the focus. France benefits from a more sizeable Afro presence than the majority of European countries. It is also, by its history, more solidly established on the African continent. Lastly, of all the nations in the world, France is the only one to claim an ideal of fraternity, which obliges it to act accordingly. As long as it continues to proclaim its desire for fraternity, it will have to rise to the occasion, and it will remain the privileged space to see the actualization of Afropea.

In France, as in the rest of the world, there is worrisome rumbling in the air. It seems that French people of European descent would endeavour to persist in their own being, to preserve their identity, to see themselves reflected in the faces they see on the metro during rush hour. There are outcries against population replacement. People are alarmed that immigrants and their descendants are supplanting the indigenous population, more and more every day. There are fears that the growing sub-Saharan population will soon make mincemeat of Europe. A new language names the drama: replacism, immigrant colonization or invasion. Never is a word uttered about the French presence in the south of the Sahara, the presence of businesses, for instance, whose operations nip local ambitions in the bud—and sometimes even take over whole sectors of the economy.

How many people in France know that the multinational retail group Auchan opened its first store in Senegal in 2015 and now has some thirty supermarkets there? Who in France worries about the plight of small Senegalese shopkeepers defeated by this giant of mass distribution with its voracious appetite?[4] Who questioned the legitimacy of the Le Monde Group when it announced in the autumn of 2015 its ambition to make *Le Monde Afrique* into the leading pan-African magazine?[5] The list is long but we shall stick to those two examples; after all the zeal of French capitalism in Africa is not really our subject here. The question should however interest those who complain of being overrun by Africa. Let us close this discussion with a reminder that the French are in no position to demand that people settling in their country adopt their customs and language, and give their children French names.

---

4 '"Auchan dégage": un collectif lutte contre l'implantation de l'enseigne au Sénégal' ['Auchan releases': A collective fights against the brand's establishment in Senegal], France 3 Régions / Hauts de France, 18 October 2018: https://-bit.ly/3LurImj (last accessed on 15 September 2023).

5 Nicolas Madelaine, '"Le Monde" veut devenir le premier media panafricain francophone' [*Le Monde* wants to become the first French-speaking pan-African media, *Les Échos*, 19 October 2015.

When they are in their former colonies, the French of only European descent speak their own language, spend decades in a region without learning a single idiom, send their children to French schools and never give them local names unless they are particularly eccentric. Sometimes they enter these countries without visas, which enables paedophiles and other criminals to profit without compunction from the rampant indigence. The French will receive in their homeland what they give others. When it comes to assimilation, they are continually setting an example. Wherever they are in the world, even in the European countries bordering France, their first reflex is to form a community, make sure there will be no lack of cheese and that they can get by without having to learn a foreign language.

Their invasion of Brooklyn spawned a neighbourhood called Little France,[6] which calls to mind the way the European invaders in the past named the territories they conquered in the Americas. They had come to recreate the land of their ancestors. On the lands of other peoples. Westernity is, if not a condition, at the least a habitus, which can be manifested between Westerners too. Even when it is not indispensable to learn another language, the French congregate in an area marked out by their compatriots. This is the case in Ixelles, one of the municipalities of Brussels, where they account for 14 per cent of the population, with more than 11,000 of the 83,000 residents. With the French lycée of Brussels filled to capacity, the opening of a second lycée was announced in 2019 in the municipality of

---

6 Mildrade Cherfils, 'À Brooklyn, "la petite France" a tout de la grande' [In Brooklyn, 'little France' has everything the big one has], *Courrier International*, 21 August 2013.

Uccle, another Gallic stronghold in the Belgian capital.[7] It seems that even when settled in a country that is European and Francophone, the French cringe at the mere thought of their offspring having a different course of studies.

The point is to enjoy all the advantages offered by the chosen environment without being affected by it. Lending but not giving oneself. And yet that is what is demanded from others, in particular when they come from Africa. The French go to Africa too. A lot. You can earn a better living there than in France. And the question of assimilation is not even on the table. Travellers from the North are sure that their presence will be to the benefit of the South, the mere fact that they deign to breathe the air will be taken as a token of consideration. If the 'civilizing mission' has become a historical expression, the behaviour that it induced persists in many forms, and this regardless of the political persuasion of the parties concerned. The world in which we live is largely Westernized, politically, economically, technologically, and so on. This is not insignificant. Particular identities resist here and there, but who would venture to claim that in the end the aforementioned domains do not influence the way of being?

International institutions exhibit a Western structure. Their mode of functioning does not draw on the differing sensibilities of their members. The sole concession made to this diversity is the use of interpreters and translators, and even this does not address sub-Saharans, given that their ancestral languages are not taken

7 Simon Souris, 'Un second "lycée français" ouvrira ses portes à Uccle' [A second 'French high school' will open its doors in Uccle], *L'Écho*, 14 March 2019.

into account. International legal texts do not draw on the different conceptions of justice that human societies developed, and no one wonders about what the pooling of diverse practices and knowledge would have produced. Everyone does as they wish in their own country, it being understood that international regulations apply to all who have ratified the conventions by which they are bound. Understandably, those who travel from the world's point of origin, as they see it, do so with the sense, even unconscious, of possessing the key.

Grumblings from French identitarians and all those who see fit to join the plaintive chorus of fallen conquerors arouse dismay. What, one wonders, could possibly have resulted from the colonial adventure and from its thinly veiled continuations? What future could all this spell for humankind? How could it have escaped even the average mind that one cannot possess all those invaded and subjugated worlds without also becoming their property? As the saying goes, the things you own end up owning you. Setting out to storm the world, conqueror-Europe delivered itself to it. The phenomenon of migration that many in Europe would like to contain was predictable. And unstoppable.

Of course one knew they would come—the sons and daughters of those who, like Grande Royale,[8] were seeking to learn 'how to conquer without being right'. If the invasion that people in France complain about were indeed taking place, wouldn't it be a sign of the success, in so many ways, of the people who, heeding only their

---

8 Character from Cheikh Hamidou Kane's novel *Ambiguous Adventure* (Katherine Falls trans.) (Oxford: Heinemann, 1962).

appetites, threw themselves on lands around the world without being invited? Those whom these distant populations did not choose to welcome now insist on choosing who can step foot on French soil. Why not? A sovereign state has the right to apply the policy that suits it. However, given that the sovereignty of all states is not equal, it seems difficult to ensure true reciprocity.

A French passport opens the doors to more than a hundred countries without the need for a visa. It would be common knowledge if citizens of, say, Mozambique or Colombia enjoyed the same privilege of entry into France. That this is not the case is proof that some states are more sovereign than others. In the postcolonial period, all nations have entered a politico-economic environment governed by the West and characterized by skewed international relations and interactions between human groups. The less powerful have to renounce the right that others enjoy to come and go unimpeded. They should be content to stand by without a peep and watch others live, barely daring to wonder when they will be entitled to do the same.

Those who wish to choose their visitors want them to be wealthy. Then, they will turn a blind eye to their customs, religion and colour. They are welcome to buy palace hotels in Paris, the biggest football clubs, rename the Prix de l'Arc de Triomphe, if they like, with no reaction from the very people who are intent on persisting in their own being while liquidating symbols of identity. We have not forgotten Muammar Gaddafi's Bedouin tent pitched in the gardens of Hôtel de Marigny, where the Libyan leader gave his audiences. France was already panhandling on the street. The

Guide of the Revolution of Libya had just signed ten billion euros worth of contracts and was counting on benefitting from the outlay. Some people objected. There was no dearth of arguments against it, but Almighty Moolah demanded its share of genuflections. And everyone complied.

The powerless and the penniless will always have a dubious culture and the colour that goes with it. They will serve as punching bags for the inextricable dilemma that is a way of life in France: is one governed by the principles one professes or guided by naked greed? It seems that the choice was made long ago. But because it went in the direction that we know and because no one can claim ignorance at a time when images travel around the planet in the blink of an eye, a way must be found not to hit rock bottom. In one's own eyes, since the others are not fools. Sub-Saharan Africa still offers immense possibilities in this regard, for internal and external reasons. There, one can flex one's muscles, speak out, give lessons in all areas, act as if sub-Saharans didn't see, like everyone else, that one spends one's time working the streets before coming to upbraid them. The king has no clothes but he's still holding a sceptre, that's the main thing.

Since sub-Saharan Africa is associated with indigence, incompetence and impotence, the human groups marked by it culturally and physically are the target of a very particular kind of racism. The Arabs, or those perceived to be Arab (meaning, all Muslims, be they from the Orient or North Africa . . . no one cares about distinctions), are feared. When I first came to France, hatred of North Africans would be expressed without mincing words. In a demonstration of sympathy for the young immigrant I was at the time, people would ask me all sorts of questions about my hair, show interest in the structure of my sub-Saharan living quarters (perhaps a tree whose trunk had been hollowed out by my parents), and inquire about how I had travelled to France (swinging from vine to vine, perhaps), before feeling the need to let me know that Blacks did not really pose a problem, whereas Arabs, on the other hand ... Whether they be rich or poor, the hostility towards them stems from the certainty that they are genetically programmed for conquest—hence for insubordination—that they are cunningly waiting for the right moment, that they will draw their dagger from the sheath when the time is ripe and that they will choose a com-bination of suicide and massacres over capitulation.

Meanwhile anti-Semitism appears to be an ancient cultural trait in the country. Since the Middle Ages when the Jews were executed in a place in Paris known as the Île aux Juifs, anti-Semitism has taken on many faces. In our time, it is often attributed to young residents of French housing-development projects, but they are far from being the only guilty parties. Although members of the majority group who hate Jews nowadays refrain from violent acts, the sentiment is nevertheless very much alive. And it is not only a religious matter, even though this question persists in the writing of certain highly appreciated essayists in nationalist circles. Well-known figures guard the flame of the country's anti-Semitic tradi-tion. These gentlemen are of an advanced age but that does not weaken their determination and their audience is often much younger, which ensures the passing on of the torch. Dark powers are attributed to Jews. The fear that they inspire is anchored in the idea that it is impossible to really know and hence control the power they supposedly wield. Somewhat like the Arabs, at bottom, but with a difference in method, and with the huge advantage of not physically standing out and of belonging to the West whose thinking they strongly contributed to forging. Nationalist circles equate the latter aspect with a corruption of intellectual and political identity. The most ardent anti-Semites dream of an unlikely alliance with the Arabs to solve the problem once and for all.

I discovered how offensive Asians found society's prejudices against them when I began meeting Asian readers of my books. Before the recent coronavirus pandemic, no one spoke much any more of the Yellow Peril, since the menace was seen as coming from sub-Saharans. Yet the stereotypes and hostile discourses about Asians had not disappeared for all that, and the pandemic made the old demons rear their ugly heads. 'Yellow peril' and 'yellow alert' were expressions used in France to speak of the coronavirus.[9] Asians living in the country were targets of racist behaviour. French citizens of Asian descent began speaking up against the racism they experience. To give just one example, Grace Ly, whose Chinese parents came to France fleeing the Khmer Rouge in Cambodia, is now known for her fight against discrimination. She has focused attention on the hyper-sexualization of Asian women and pointed out the impossibility of positive racism. Prejudices are always

9 *L'Obs*, 'Le "Courrier picard" s'excuse après sa une raciste sur l'"Alerte jaune"' [The *Courrier picard* apologizes after its racist take on the 'Yellow Alert'], 27 January 2020.

reductionist. Whether the Asian body inspires disgust or is considered sexually available, the rejection, as in the two aforementioned cases, stems from the autonomy exhibited through community solidarities. In this case too, it is an indomitable force, an energy that cannot be appropriated.

The groups mentioned above seem more or less established on the community level. They would be able to mobilize a variety of resources for the collective and leave aside their internal disagreements in the event that they needed to defend themselves. It may only be an impression, but it feeds deeply ingrained beliefs. On the other hand, sub-Saharans and Afro-descendants are seen as repositories of a culture of pleasure that makes them insatiable consumers, easily corruptible, ready to sell mother and father to buy cars, ornaments and tailored suits. Racism targeting sub-Saharans and Afro-descendants, the only ones designated by the supposed colour of their skin, speaks of a reduction of human beings to their appearance, to the life of the body, to primal needs. Because the inventors of the Black race situated themselves at the other end of the spectrum in becoming White, any identification is compromised. People of sub-Saharan descent, especially the men, may also inspire fear. But it is not the emotion prompted by being confronted with another human being who is also capable of domination by virtue of his intellectual qualities. The Black provokes the kind of fright that an unexpected encounter with a wild beast would trigger, thus unleashing the most irrational of reactions. The cases of police brutality, which are legion, are proof of this, and one is struck speechless by the description of the events that lead to mutilation or death. Fear of the Black sometimes resembles what the sight of a giant cockroach might provoke: the kind of disgust that triggers murderous impulses. The Black is a figment of the conjurer's imagination. He represents an imaginary threat. We know who is in command and it surely is not he.

When it comes to sub-Saharans or Afro-descendants, phenotype blindness and the spontaneous identification with every human being is not by any means guaranteed. French society pretends to recognize only individuals and not the ethnic groups from which they come, but it actually does not see itself reflected in the face of Blacks. It does not identify them as people upholding values that it prides itself on embodying. They are not figures of the universal, even negatively as are all the others, those that have now become customers and competitors in strategic areas. Those who successfully imposed an imperialist religion and dominated European territories.[10] Those who were once colonized but who now have sovereign control of their resources. All those whose memory ignores capture, transoceanic deportations and colonial slavery—the succession of events that gave birth to the Black, embodiment of failure, dispossession and powerlessness.

The seemingly positive prejudices that people have towards those of sub-Saharan descent do not mitigate the significance of the above. They all relate to entertainment. The suffering of Blacks is in itself a spectacle. Do they not set it admirably to music? Do

10 The Ottoman Empire extended into a Hungarian province from around 1540 to 1680. Andalusia had a long Arab-ruled period from the eighth to the fifteenth centuries. Part of the Caucasus was Islamized as early as the seventh century.

they not dance it incomparably well? And it is because the humanity of the people that history blackened remains stamped with the seal of inferiority that it is impossible to identify with them. Appearing in blackface to masquerade as sub-Saharans at the Dunkirk carnival or as Harlem Globetrotters underscores this distancing. Otherwise, the costume would suffice. It would not be necessary to colour your skin. This is an element of the disguise because it is significant and it has to be removable so as to regain a human face. With the exception of cases when people disguise themselves as animals to entertain theme-park visitors, such a thing is rarely done. To imitate human beings usually involves the use of accessories that the imitated persons themselves could dispense with. Skin does not fall into this category, which is what makes the practice so aggressive.

Faced with the history of colonial conquests, and more particularly of slavery, the lie that prevails in France of blindness to skin colour unravels. That is where the refusal to see oneself in the other is most flagrant. All you have to do is bring up the question of slavery for critics of communitarianism to suddenly discover that they are White, irremediably and essentially so. The values that are proclaimed day in and day out are no longer in effect. If they were, they would see a reflection of themselves in those who embody these values. They would stand by their side, firmly. That never happens. Even when demonstrating extreme bad faith, it would be well-nigh impossible not to see that in this story it is the oppressed, the enslaved who have turned their lives into a relentless quest for liberty, equality and fraternity. They are France in what it has that is most noble and such as it aspires to present itself to the world. But they are Black. They were construed as such to be cast out from the human family, never to be a brother but only this other whose skin cannot be inhabited in consciousness, meaning not through masks but by way of a deep understanding of their experience.

The enslaved is Black, which says nothing about the person's complexion. On the other hand, it is telling of the place assigned to him and occupied thereafter by his descendants. And this Blackness that is not a colour signifies degradation and powerlessness. That is what people want to distance themselves from at all costs. To be able to maintain their claim of embodying the country's values without having to accept responsibility for the person's status. That is the reason that, suddenly, one is White. For even though the White of history is degraded through the violence inflicted on the Black invented for this sole purpose, the latter nonetheless brings proof of the former's power. And power is the motivator. Little does it matter that one's reputation is built on bloody hands and mountains of corpses. Power wards off threats, precisely because one's capacity for cruelty has been well demonstrated.

Faced with the history of colonial conquests and slavery, one is hard put to speak of citizens of the world or universal humanity. All that remains is the manufacture of race, its motivations and the returns that the proper annuitant of Westernity reaps. That is what makes the mention of this history so intolerable, a culpability in regard to a symbolic and material heritage that one simply cannot give up for the sake of fraternizing, which means starting by doing justice. Anyway, enough has been done already, hasn't it? After all,

France redeemed itself by abolishing slavery. However, the fact is that the abolitions of slavery were first and foremost the result of the ongoing struggles of the oppressed, which is something that French discourse all too often tends to elide. Furthermore, the argument reveals its dishonesty when you perceive that slavery was abolished to pave the way for the project of colonizing Africa where the populations would be put to work, even forcibly.[11] It was not until 1946 that France abolished forced labour in its West African colonies. Almost a century after the second abolition of slavery, the one in 1848 that is supposed to have cleansed France of its sins.

There is a desire to consign all this to a distant past and stop dwelling on it. But it is those who refuse to see themselves in the values rather than in the phenotype of the protagonists of history are the only ones, in reality, to live in the past. They are the ones who import it into the present, locking one and all into racial positions, and influencing minorities by their behaviour. The fact that descendants of sub-Saharans reduced to slavery are today French citizens, living in French regions, and carrying with them cultures that should be part of French heritage does not seem to make things any easier. This Afro-descendant presence that resulted from colonial slavery is downplayed in all respects. To insist that it be revealed, owned and accepted in the family album would amount to demanding repentance.

This goes to show the tenacity of the attachment to the perpetrator rather than to the victim. It also demonstrates the strength

---

11 Jean-François Zorn, 'L'étrange destin de l'abolition de l'esclavage' [The strange fate of the abolition of slavery], *Autres Temps* 22 (1989): 54–63.

of the racial imaginary, even its centrality, in a society that claims to be free of it. Another illustration of this phenomenon is to be found in the positive connotation that the word *métissage* tends to have in France. This term has its origin not only in racial thinking but in the very idea of inequality between races. *Métisser* (according to the French-language dictionary the *Littré*) originally meant to cross-breed ovine races for the purposes of improving the inferior breed. That the term is now applied to human beings, or more oddly to cultures, only confirms the asymmetry internalized by one and all: humans are not equal, nor are their cultures; and when cross-breeding takes place only one of the two parties benefits.

The vocabulary itself is rigged, locked into a racist mindset that is only several centuries old, but that has become so deeply ingrained that it seems impossible to get past it. We cannot continue to speak of humanity in a language that we have not rid of the violence that it conveys. We need new words to express what we have now become and what we want to be. We have to free ourselves, all of us, for history cannot be rewritten, and here we are, still imprisoned in its darkest regions. Afropea comes to open the doors of the jail. For the prison sentence to come to an end, the schemas induced by Westernity will have to be repudiated.

Sub-Saharan Africa's relations with Europe are stamped with the seal of this incarceration. One would like to think that, after all this time, the encounter between these areas of the world has actually taken place and produced its effects, some of which are appreciable. But that is jumping the gun. Whereas things can go well for individuals, this is not the case on a broader scale. And individuals themselves cannot always avoid the intrusion into their private lives of the political aspects of the relationship between the two areas. A shock took place, a collision of sorts that still keeps the two regions from really looking at each other. A relationship does exist, but it is tainted from the outset, too imbalanced for us to be satisfied with.

What needs to be developed now are new ways of keeping company with one another, ways of being in the world that are productive for both parties, that allow each to thrive without the other suffering as a result. This is a challenge. This may be in the realm of the utopian, but let us put to work whatever we can. Our resources would be slim if we were to rely on common sense alone. We must aim higher, dare to think differently in order to repair a bond that will not be broken for objective reasons. To the anxiety-inducing reality that is ours, let us respond with the radicality of a new path, which calls our presuppositions and our habits into question. Afropea offers this. I propose to show how it can dispel the 'colonial melancholia' that inhabits France.[12]

The interpretation that I intend to develop of Afropea does not coincide with the way the term was formulated by the people who first identified with it. Yet the word is here. A true grasp of its meaning tells us of the project it harbours. Each of my assertions about what the Afropean approach and sensibility are and are not will proceed from the designation and its structure. I will be saying the thing by building on the word, independently of the trajectories

---

12 I'm borrowing the idea of 'colonial melancholia' from Paul Gilroy, *Postcolonial Melancholia* (New York: Columbia University Press, 2004).

of those who have appropriated the term to define themselves and those who have deviated at times from the path mapped by it. What follows is a discussion that does not rely on a precise conceptual framework, a political reflection that a formal Afropean manifesto could very well contest or enhance. It is the sub-Saharan in me that is concerned with the fate of Afropeans, with what they contribute to the societies of which they are a part and, of course, to Africa. I will also be bringing up aspects of diasporic history, as Afropea is the latest of the Afro-descendant categories and has much to offer them through its originality. More than being a mere identity-based approach, Afropea seems to me to formulate a demand and convey a critique of the functioning of the two universes that constitute it.

A Brief History of the Term

In the beginning, Afropea has to do with sound. David Byrne, co-founder of the band Talking Heads, coined the term in the early 1990s. He used it to designate a fictional continent that allowed for the exploration through music of the influence of African cultures on European sensibilities. The initiative was a worthwhile one and Byrne recognized that the meeting between peoples left none untouched. Three albums, entitled *Adventures in Afropea*, were compiled with sonorities emanating from the mutual impregnation of cultures and released on Byrne's Luaka Bop label.

The idea escaped its devisor to acquire new meaning. Europeans of sub-Saharan descent in particular appropriated it to name not a virtual space but a living reality, the movement of their identity. Afropea thus gave birth to Afropean, a contraction of Afro-European. The morphology of the neologism evokes a coupling. The bonding that is imposed here defeats the desires for distancing, eliminates the reasons for which one could want to avoid dealing with or having anything to do with the other. The appellation is troubling. The world in which we live still favours national spaces. These are the territories in relation to which individuals are expected to define themselves. And most people do opt for a definition based on nationality or country of birth. They may then go on to provide further specifications, indicating a region of the territory.

Those who call themselves Afropeans, and who may speak French, or Norwegian, or German or English, propose a world-view that is not tied to a national space, though they do not deny belonging to one. The designation is remarkable in this regard and warrants closer examination. The validity of a term that obliterates any reference to the nation can be questioned, but it evinces an ambition. Saying you are Afropean is not the same as saying you are Senegalo-French or Afro-French. It is seeing bigger; it is embracing a greater number.

It was the voices of artists that introduced Afropea to me. The year 1991, which was the year I came to France, also saw the release of the first record of the Belgian group Zap Mama whose founder Marie Daulne and her sister Anita presented themselves as Afropeans. The combo's album *Adventures in Afropea, Vol. I* is the most well-known of the trilogy compiled by Byrne. Zap Mama set out to revitalize sub-Saharan culture, ensure that the oldest creators of this part of the world would be seen as such, and mix musical elements from different continents. The group wanted an Afropean singularity to be heard in their sounds and they remain pioneers in this respect.

It is impossible to discuss the emergence of the word Afropean in the francophone world without mentioning Marie and Anita Daulne. They may not have produced a theoretical discourse as such, but deep thinking nurtured their music. Born in sub-Saharan Africa, raised in Europe from their early childhood, they seem to have received a strong sub-Saharan heritage from their Congolese mother, especially concerning women's education. Thanks to her, they felt richer and stronger than the Europeans who did not have the privilege of a sub-Saharan ancestry. For Marie, the sensibility transmitted to her by her mother was an antidote to Europe's mental pathologies, liberating the individual from the weight of social rigidities. In their respective areas—stage performance for the one, teaching and singing for the other—the Daulne sisters hoped to develop a soteriology through music, for themselves and for others.

The 1990s saw the term Afropean take hold in music circles where it was first born. This would not necessarily give rise to a clear expression of identity specificity or an emphasis on a particular cultural heritage. References, when they existed, were not Afropean. This may have been due to a lack of knowledge about the Afro-descendant presence in Europe and hence a somewhat accidental treatment, *in absentia*. These artists' ignorance of an Afropean past betrays the dissimulation by European societies of a part of their history. One can also see in the lack of strictly Afropean themes a way of indicating that there are none, that the human being is the subject and that it is above all a question of the human condition. The truth is no doubt there and elsewhere.

In 1995, the English rap group Cash Crew released *From an Afropean Perspective*. The album came out in France on the label Vogue. The article presenting it in the French magazine *Les Inrockuptibles* started with the following sentence: 'Arguing that

Black communities living in the different countries of Europe have more in common with each other than with their national compatriots, Cash Crew establishes the concept of Afropean.'[1]

The author of the piece was mistaken about the term's genesis, but what he indicated about Cash Crew's motivations is interesting. Afropea opts here to relegate national territory to a secondary position so as to prioritize the human connections that impart meaning to this ethnicity. What counts is the particular life experience of Afro-descendants in Europe. The historical trajectories differ insofar as some countries were colonial powers and others were not. Nonetheless, a similarity remains: Afropeans are deprived of representation in a country that, in spite of being theirs, presents itself to the world without mentioning them, without letting them embody it. To their compatriots of only European descent, Afropeans are foreigners, and they are expected to justify being there among them, and even being at all. In addition, they bear a different cultural heritage and do not wish to dismiss it. If this heritage resides in them solely in the form of traces, since not all parents have transmitted it in the same way, their consciousness of its particularities prompts them to forge themselves in an alternative, even transgressive, fashion.

France has difficulty understanding them. The waves of immigration from Europe are compared with those from former colonies and the latter are found wanting for resisting assimilation. Some point an accusing finger at particular sub-Saharan cultures whose

1 Damien Conaré, 'From an Afropean Perspective', *Les Inrockuptibles*, 30 September 1995: https://bit.ly/4839emv (last accessed on 23 December 2023).

very nature would prevent integration.[2] Beyond the fact that capitalism points a gun at populations the world over and that sub-Saharans are among the hordes that it throws out of their countries, colonial history makes these paths singular. Sub-Saharans did not choose the French Republic. It invited itself over to their homelands and quickly practised a type of colonization that did not simply aim at trading and exploiting the resources of these distant territories but at expanding its own. France turned its colonies into an extension of itself.

Those countries, fabricated from scratch, were France. Let us not go back over the concrete modalities of appropriation of the space and the people, as each country concerned had its own particular French history. The Ivory Coast's differs from Cameroon's, and so on. My point here is the following: if one wants to dominate over the long term, violence alone—be it physical or psychological—is not enough. To be successful in this enterprise, one must take possession of minds and infiltrate cultures. Bring the victims of aggression to actively collaborate in their own downfall. For this purpose, an elite close to the colonialists is established and educated in the colonial school. They are given work and a place envied by the masses. By the comfort they enjoy and the lifestyle they adopt, the colonized bourgeoisie promote colonial culture. They live to resemble their masters. The ardour they put into this combines with the colonizer's efforts to produce a desire for France in one and all.

2 Hugues Lagrange, *Le Déni des cultures* [The denial of cultures] (Paris: Seuil, 2010).

I know what I am talking about, having had a front seat to observe the phenomenon when I refused to go to the French lycée that my parents proposed that I attend. I had seen the profound change in attitude on the part of a cousin who had started secondary studies in the French school a few years earlier. Now she was sitting at the right hand of God and she barely addressed a word to my sisters and me. And this after having spent our childhood at each other's neighbouring homes. I was ten, but I could already see what was wrong, the private drama of this superior caste. This colonized bourgeoisie, which stands as a representation of the North in the South, is active in all sub-Saharan countries. Its quasi-acculturation has so far guaranteed it the best places in society. Aside from this, sub-Saharans are used to their leaders looting and placing their stolen capital abroad. Investing it in French real estate, squandering it on French luxury products. Seeing this, it is understandable that some find themselves attracted to this destination. They have been conditioned for this.

The Afropean perspective envisaged by Cash Crew was more akin to the invention to which sub-Saharan Africa must resolve itself in our time than to the exhumation of an ancestral past denigrated by Europe. Accepting the idea of being identity mutants, of not being reducible to disturbing nationalities. Such a political and poetic approach was not easy to pursue in a hostile European society. *From an Afropean Perspective* was Cash Crew's second and last album before its members split up.

In France, Les Nubians was the group that drew attention to the Afropean designation. Hélène and Célia Faussart presented themselves as Afropeans, something that France didn't understand at the time. It was in the United States that their first album *Princesses nubiennes* (1998) was certified a gold album.[3] They were nominated for the Grammys in the 'Best Urban/Alternative Performance' category. Even Americans who did not know French understood the message conveyed through the style of the music, the collaborations with stars and the historical figures mentioned in the songs. The artists' look was also a tool to appeal to a public in search of visual performances of identity. Les Nubians embodied the imagery developed in their lyrics. Like other Afropean artists, they recognized having been influenced by Black America, as France offered Afro-descendants few models. In their early years, they were exposed to African American images, more recurrent, more attractive and more valued than Afropean representations.

Many others after Zap Mama, Cash Crew and Les Nubians adopted the word Afropean, either to define their identity or to describe the style of their creations. In France, the duo DjeuhDjoah & Lieutenant Nicholson call their music Afropean. The Belgian Baloji defines himself as Afropean. Other artistic areas have

3 One could hardly claim that Les Nubians were rejected by the French public or by music circles in their own country only because they were Black. The truth is more complex and certainly has to do with their strong Afrocentric stances at the start. Their collaboration with the first-rate artist Jean-Louis Aubert ('Univers', 1998) is nevertheless worth recalling. And, more importantly, the 90s saw the appearance of another duo of Black girls that had stunning and well-deserved success with soul-pop songs performed in French. Laura and Chris Mayne, the Martiniquans of the group Native, won the award for the most promising group of the year at the Victoires de la Musique in 1994. Four hundred thousand copies of their first album, *Native* (1994), were sold in France.

followed suit. In France, Eva Doumbia staged *Afropéenes*, a play about Afro-descendant women in France, based on two of my texts. Doumbia is also the initiator of Massilia Afropea, a festival in Marseille dedicated to Afropean creations and lifestyles. Cultural circles outside France have grown interested in the notion too. In September 2014, an Austrian festival titled Afropea Now! explored Afropean identities and cultural productions. In June 2019 and again in February 2020, the Royal Flemish Theatre, KVS, hosted *Afropean / Human Being*, the first play written by British poet Sukina Doublas.

Academics have not failed to seize upon the term. The interest in this new category of Afro-descendance has given rise to research work and colloquiums, including the Afroeuropeans Network Conference created in 2006. Since 2009, it has been organized every two years by researchers and artists from different countries in Europe. Social networks and the digital world at large evidence this sensibility too. A case in point is *AFRØPEAN—Adventures in Black Europe*, the multimedia journal founded by photographer Johny Pitts. Like many others, Pitts—whose father is African American and mother British—adopts an understanding of Afropea that is not immediately related to sub-Saharan Africa. As the title of the online journal indicates, the focus is mainly on highlighting the experience of Blacks in Europe. In European France, this could be the approach of people with Caribbean ties. This is the case for Marie-Julie Chalu, creator of the Afropea platform.

As we can see, the denomination is subject to a dynamism that, while not muddling it completely, may make it difficult to grasp. I reiterate here the definition given as a preamble, in an attempt not to freeze what cannot be, but to insist on the particularities of the construction of the self—in childhood and adolescence—in a minority situation, in a space that has the latitude to present itself to the world without mentioning the Afro-descendant presence. Not only because it was reduced to silence or even obliterated, as it was in certain Latin American countries such as Argentina, Mexico or Peru, but because the territory in question has, in fact, had a long history that does not include in any significant way people of sub-Saharan descent.

The French Urgency

In France, the most radical nationalist movements, often led by individuals who are surprisingly young, subscribe to White communitarianism and call for a territorial partition that would enable a definitive racial separation. In such a context, Afropea has something to say. Indeed, it is also its presence, increasingly uninhibited, and its social successes, though still few in number, that provoke the malaise among those who hold onto race as their prime capital and ultimate refuge. Certain long-propagated discourses and representations had guaranteed for them the inferiority of sub-Saharans and Afro-descendants, and this gave them a sense of power. A fringe of White French youth literally vomits the model of society that their elders propose. In identity-based movements like the Suavelos,[1] they loudly proclaim their rejection of the multiracial society, their opposition to francophony, which obliges them to share their language, and their confidence in the superiority of Whites.

There is something pitiful about the agitation of these young people arming themselves after the battle is over. The future is

---

1 Adrien Sénécat, 'La galaxie Suavelos, vitrine d'un racisme décomplexé' [The Suavelos galaxy, a showcase of uninhibited racism], *Le Monde*, 11 September 2019.

knocking at the door and they are conducting rear-guard warfare. There is surely a poetry of sorts to seeing them waltzing with ghosts and dreaming of a France that drew its dying breath before they let out their first cry. Suavelos is supposed to mean both 'welcome' and 'godspeed' in the language of the Gauls. It is not surprising that the organization's founders chose a name indicating the ancient character of the White presence on French soil. It is also understandable that, as they do not know the dead language of their Celtic ancestors, they would grasp at its lowest hanging branches to mark their filiation. The name they chose illustrates the pathetic nature of their project and prompts unfavourable speculations about the group's future. Imagine that Black Lives Matter, for instance, decided to call itself 'What's up' or 'Take it easy'? This reference comes to mind because it seems that the Suavelos want to remind us that White lives should matter too. The situation would be as follows: supposedly French people of only European descent have to hug the walls, are no longer to be heard or seen anywhere and are seriously discriminated against. The members of Suavelos mainly point to a plague that must be resisted in the hopes of fighting it more effectively later when Whites, conscious of the tragedy that awaits them, will be more numerous and uninhibited.

This bane eating away at Western societies, especially in France, has a name: globalized leftism. The latter takes the form of antiracism, feminism, an acceptance of marginal sexualities, but also of internationalism, seen as a form of statelessness that characterizes an elite favourable to the migratory invasion. These new militants see the French right as essentially antiracist and the

45

Rassemblement National[2] itself as tending towards leftism. Other elements connected to economic liberalism, for example, could be added to the list, but the above-mentioned sum up the problem that Suavelos and their acolytes intend to battle to the point of triumph or extinction. At least they will have gone down with honours. To be frank, there would be a semblance of elegance to their patriotism and love for their own that would be worthy of respect if its source and highest expression did not proceed from the rejection of the other.

These young people are not merely fervent racists. They are also supremacists who do not shy away from raising—on days when the idea of partition appears to them in all its ridiculous splendour—the possibility of a technological war to counter the colonial invasion. One wonders what the provenance could be of the metals needed to manufacture the lethal instruments meant to eradicate harmful human beings once and for all. One would like to ask them how it is that given the superiority of Whites in everything, they could be colonized by the wretched of the earth. Isn't it surprising that inferior peoples, of dubious genetic heritage and low intellectual quotient, could constitute a threat to the demigods terrified by the dark dusk that is descending on their world?

Such is, nowadays, the posterity of the conquerors: fearful, lost, desirous of retracing in the opposite direction the path that led their forebears to storm the world. Does God store up the punishment

---

2 Known as the Front National until 2018, and led by Marine Le Pen until 2022, the Rassemblement National (National Rally) is the largest far-right political party in France. [Trans.]

of the father for his children?[3] The biblical question haunts those who realize today that trying to appropriate the world condemns them to becoming its property, and that their ancestors set out in the past on a path of no return. Not only because they wanted to spread to the far corners of the Earth, to possess every square millimetre of it, but also because they created needs that cannot be satisfied without the resources of other territories and other populations. The Westernization of the world was accomplished at this price: the presence of the other within the self, definitively.

Who would even think of doing without such colonial commodities as coffee, cacao and tea? The first meal of the day, even in the homes of the staunchest nationalists, testifies to the long incorporation of the other in oneself. It was during the period of European conquests and slavery that colonial products were integrated into the daily lives of the French and they quickly became indispensable. They became so familiar that one forgot the humans exploited far away to obtain these delicacies. In 1792, humble Parisians attacked the houses of sugar merchants and looted their reserves. Not a thought did they have for the insurgents of Saint-Domingue—which became Haiti—whose revolution, which started in August 1791, caused the penury and price increase. Yet, the invisible body of the enslaved, their suffering and the resources that they mobilized to counter the violence against them were ingested by sugar consumers. Ever since, the flesh of the ones never ceases to mix with that of the others. This process is much deeper than the mixing usually designated by the term *métissage*. The

---

3 Job 21:19.

Parisians of the past were not worse than the crowds that line up at dawn in front of the Apple Stores without a thought for the Congolese whose labour and often death irrigate the latest technological toy. The relationship between peoples, albeit dysfunctional and asymmetrical, is established. It is not the hoped-for convergence, but its reality is undeniable. No amount of complaining and grumbling can change that.

Orania, a small exclusively Afrikaner town in South Africa founded after the end of apartheid, is an ideal for the members of Suavelos. They might be able to achieve at least that, to find an enclave somewhere to hole up and protect themselves from unwanted guests. They will have to search outside of France for this White paradise, look for it in a country that did not reduce so many sub-Saharans to slavery, nor colonize a good part of the planet. These neo-nationalists with little money do not hesitate to break open their piggy banks to make donations to Orania. In the meantime, until they build their replica of this racially pure city, their fantasies turn to Hungary or the Baltic countries, given that Western Europe has sullied itself too much in welcoming those it otherwise continues to pillage without compunction.

This new nationalist wave is unsettling. It emanates from people originating in the majority group who act in ways more common among minorities. Because it is more extensive than the mention here of one of its divisions alone might lead one to suppose, the new nationalist trend provides a glimpse in France and in Europe of a future of divisions at best and clashes at worst. I am not speaking of the frictions necessary for change, of the kind of conversations that society still refuses to have, as the mere mention of its colonial history is perceived as compelling it to confess its guilt. What I am referring to is an incendiary situation, as no one is willing to turn the other cheek or even extend a hand. Already, France is imploding.

Rejection of the other and outright racism are not likely to elicit the friendliest of reactions. A collapse of humanity is looming on the horizon. Politicians and the media have made the far-right viewpoints, which are thriving in the majority group, seem run-of-the-mill. Minorities cannot be expected to set their sights high or demonstrate a desire for fraternity when the majority group fails to do so. Trying to ward off this fate and open up new paths requires more than sticking to the ideas of hybridity and mixing to which we are accustomed. The time has come to introduce more radical methods, to stop deconstructing and to assert that what is needed is to build something else. The issue is as imperative as climate change, which is not a crisis.[4] It is not a passing thing; it is the new state of the world to which we must adapt by saving what can be saved.

The planet does not need us. What we express in our concern for the environment is that the Earth remains habitable for us. What is the interest, at bottom, if relations of domination and spoliation continue? If the refusal to recognize one's humanity in the other's persists? Relations between peoples and between communities, and the way that colonial history can at last be put behind us are

---

4 The author uses 'crisis' to denote an urgent but temporary situation, one that is likely to end. While climate change is undeniably pressing, it can be argued that the term crisis understates its long-term and potentially irreversible consequences. [Ed.]

therefore crucial issues to address in the societies in question but also in the other societies that they continue to influence and with which they share the world.

My interpretation of the meanings of Afropea is not meant to provide a ready-made crisis-exit strategy. Such a survival manual, such a tool for transcending the brewing resentments and bitterness will emerge from bringing new thoughts into conversation. None of the aforementioned artists have been consulted. Since none of them produced myths—in the sense of artistic, symbolic representations— or theories on the subject, it did not seem relevant to me to solicit them. Neither have these artists highlighted Afropean memory, which is sufficiently well documented, provided one makes the effort of reading research and takes an interest in the presence of people of sub-Saharan descent in European France before the nineteenth century and the colonization of Africa. The imagination of Afropean creators in France did not draw on such figures as the Black Nun of Moret[5] or the Black soldiers of Maurice de Saxe, Marshall of France.[6] *Rape of a Negress* (1632), a painting by Christiaen Van Couwenbergh in the Musée de Beaux Arts, Strasbourg, did not attract their attention. The sight of a painting like *Madeleine de la Martinique et Sa Mère* elicited no artistic

---

5 Louise Marie-Thérèse (1664–1732), a Benedictine nun in the abbey of Moret-sur-Loing. See 'Alain Decaux discuses La Mauresse de Moret', ORTF, 17 July 1969: https://bit.ly/3VLMgeg (last accessed on 13 October 2023).

6 André Corvisier, 'Les soldats noirs du maréchal de Saxe. Le problème des Antillais et Africains sous les armes en France au xviiie siècle' [The Black soldiers of Marshal de Saxe: The problem of Antilleans and Africans under arms in France in the eighteenth century], *Outre-Mers Revue d'histoire* 101 (1968): 367–413.

response. Madeleine, a little Black girl who suffered from vitiligo, was painted by Le Masurier in 1782. She is shown with her mother, a young slave or servant attentive to the girl's first steps. This striking painting belongs to the Museum of Natural History in Paris. Much could be said and written about the very fact that this is where it is located.

The reason why Afropean creators have disdained certain figures until recently may very well reside in the proximity of all imperialist and racist societies with the enslaving environment, from the standpoint of damage to the psyche, and hence of the relationship that one has to one's history.

Many Caribbean writers (Naipaul, Chamoiseau, Damas, etc.) have made this point: Creoles, marked by slavery and the contempt for themselves inculcated by this institution, have trouble relating to their past without shame or resentment, when they do not simply repress it.[7]

A malaise of the same nature may have prevented Afropeans from turning to figures who embodied defeat in their eyes. Owning these faces meant confronting the country's history of slavery. People of sub-Saharan descent who could be found in European France before the colonization of Africa often carried this history within them. Neither Madeleine in the Paris Museum of Natural History nor the one in the Louvre were perceived as worthwhile forebears, which is why they were abandoned to silence. For a writer, the mystery surrounding these figures is an invitation to fill the gaps in the

---

7 Dénètem Touam Bona, *Fugitif, où cours-tu?* [Fugitive, where do you run?] (Paris: PUF, 2016), p. 48.

French narrative. Fictional writing may not uncover the factual truth of unknown destinies. But it could reveal others.

Many Afropean artists have taken the easy road in turning solely to Africa, provider of kings and queens galore. Having abandoned the Afropean perspective, many experience their ethnicity as a belonging with no distinct history or discourse, a sort of exiled Africanity in Europe, a Black being encumbered by their European side. This situation is easy to explain. France has long practised a not-in-your-face, cordial form of racism, which affords hope of being accepted provided one does not dwell too much on all those stories of people having suffered a lot. You are admitted into the group in the subordinate position of a mascot, a *pote*, a 'buddy', not to be touched,[8] a somewhat backward comrade whom one is willing to civilize, a representative of the Black hyper-hotness that is transmitted from generation to generation, producing contingents of studs to ride and tigresses to tame. You have to show yourself to be nice and funny, to live your Black being with no awareness of its political nature, as if it were a physical particularity like any other: flat feet, a prominent nose, a heavy build. You have to keep quiet when you hear racist jokes so as not to offend those who are heartily laughing because it is so amusing. Letting yourself be ridiculed will be the only way of existing alongside others. Not altogether among them, but nearly, which is already something. You will have to hear yourself saying that you were *not like the others*, and therefore not concerned by the joke, since you have almost

---

8 *Touche pas à mon pote*, 'Hands off my buddy', was the slogan in the 1980s of anti-racism NGO, SOS Racisme. [Trans.]

gained access to humanity through your contact with the higher beings whose friend you are.

And that is how you behave, having internalized the social injunctions so well that you would merrily delude yourself, reassured that you are making people laugh and offending no one but yourself. It is shocking for us today to watch the sketch by Les Inconnus in which one of the trio of humourists, Pascal Légitimus, presents a South African news broadcast. In blackface, puffing up his lips to make the redness protrude, the comic speaks in a sub-Saharan accent unknown in Africa to announce the liberation of Nelson Mandela. In the context that produced this, that led to this type of self-negation, it is understandable that Afropeans retreated from the task that was theirs: that of learning about their own French history, speaking about it, instituting it, for themselves to begin with. Cordial racism is a form of manipulation that relieves one of having to spit on people oneself. Unlike outright racism, which involves self-aggrandisement, the racism practised in France, with its ambivalence, its slyness, its policy of a bird in the hand is worth more than two in the bush, annihilates all defences. Moreover it is a losing battle, since society has done all it could to make sure that one is always alone to confront it. That is the purpose of the directive to free oneself of all sense of belonging to a community, which applies only to minorities emerging from colonial history. To do one's best to prove that one is *not like the others*, to dissipate the shadow of the vindictive tribe that one might be dragging in one's wake.

Even without being staunch supremacists (and who needs to be so in a context where racism attains such levels of sophistication?), the members of the majority group are driven by a domineering worldview and afflicted by a racial unconscious that surfaces as soon as their privileges appear threatened. With its racist trolls, a cyberbullying group, the Ligue du LOL,[9] provided a good example of this in a country where the rejection of the other was no longer beating around the bush. This episode in the famous *vivre ensemble* will have at least made it clear that French minorities are not posing as victims when they speak of racism also spreading on the left. From that side of the political divide, its expression is usually condescending and paternalistic. After all, we are among those who used to have 'buddies' not to be touched. Ever since racist speech and acts were liberated during the Sarkozy years, and all cordiality removed from them, the victims of aggression no longer aspire to be mascots or nice buddies. They respond, defend themselves, demand, pronounce words like negrophobia, white supremacy, racial profiling, cultural appropriation, etc. And then, the masks fall off.

The Ligue du LOL evidenced the way in which some people can claim they are on the left merely as a means of exercising moral authority over others. They do not believe in the ideals they profess and do not live according to them. The rhetoric serves them only to occupy media space, to make sure they are in places where they

---

9 The Ligue du LOL, or League of Lots of Laughs, was a Facebook group created by a French journalist and composed of journalists, bloggers and communication professionals. Other private groups comprising thousands of racist and supremacist police personnel have been discovered on social networks since then.

wield power and can hold onto it. Ligue members have made their way into the companies that employ them, where they have risen to high positions. And they are, one and all, White. The communitarianism of which minorities are regularly accused is manifested here in no uncertain terms, since the point is to keep to themselves, to establish and preserve this *entre soi*, this being with one's own kind, racially speaking as well. This is a frequent occurrence, even a sort of unwritten rule, in a country that loathes hearing talk of systemic racism but demonstrates its skill in the matter every day.

If the French of only European descent, regardless of social class, were asked how many peers they have from minority backgrounds, the way things are would become apparent. When you are a columnist in a major media outlet, the housekeeper is not your peer. The Ligue is not a *sui generis* phenomenon. It did not give birth to itself. It was spawned by a system. An environment governed by misdirected masculine forces and by hierarchies of race, class and gender. A society driven by an innate colonialist impulse. Including in the ranks of those who call themselves leftists. The internet snipers were above suspicion. They were at the cutting edge of coolness—in fact, that was their function, their mission in life: being the great trendsetters. Yet something that was festering inside them came to a head, and it burst through the phoney progressivism. Something like an overload of Westernity gone haywire as a result of the presence of Afropea, asserting itself on the epistemic plane on the hip editorial boards of the Parisian press.

A Post-Western Way of Thinking

Afropea, whose name clearly indicates its post-national intention, seems Western because of the profile of the term's inventor and the space within which this ethnicity is deployed. I will say later why this reading is misguided, but suffice it to say for the time being that it is also because it is understood as a renunciation of Africanness in that it does not call for approval in a segment of Negrohood.[1] The designation is shunned by cultural nationalists, sub-Saharans and Afro-descendants, who see it as a form of dissociation from Africa, of claiming a multi-belonging with the sole aim of cleansing those who use the name of a historical stigma. Afropea is to their mind a manifestation of self-hatred, the display of an identity complex. There are now dedicated racialists among sub-Saharans and Afro-descendants, top-ranking essentialists who quickly gloss over the fact that these conceptions were not part of the worldview of the sub-Saharan ancestors whom they revere.

If pre-colonial Africa had been attached to a definition of human beings based on skin colour, a racial brotherhood would

---

1 An ironic and nonetheless affectionate term, which I use in my novels as well, drawing on the charming neologism coined by the African American novelist Zora Neale Hurston.

have been forged, united against common enemies during the colonial conquests. Not only did this not happen, but alliances with Europeans against other sub-Saharans were legion. Because the neighbour, who did not speak the same language and had a different name for the divinity, was not any Blacker than oneself. Because kinship was founded on other criteria. The Afro-descendants who established Liberia under the leadership of the American Colonization Society did not identify with the inhabitants of the territory, who in return did not identify with them. We know what happened next: the story of the impossible reunion that led to war a few generations later. *Blacks* and *Africans* are designations that speak of the rebuilding through colonialization of identity infrastructures south of the Sahara. They are irrelevant when it comes to describing the pre-colonial period and do not provide any insight into the sub-Saharan experience in the past. Subscribers to identity purity have internalized colonial notions to such an extent that they can no longer conceive of a project of liberation without picking the ideological pockets of the Western far right. Their logic is to sub-Saharan thinking what wax prints are to endogenous African textiles: a European fabrication so well assimilated that it becomes conflated with ancestral heritage and ends up supplanting it.

To be sure, Negritude left its mark. The necessary revalorization of colonized cultures and peoples that it set out to effect involved adhering to racial thinking. To conceive of the idea of Negritude, one had to stand by the notion of race, validate it emphatically. Afrocentricity left its mark as well. Its commitment to bringing sub-Saharans and Afro-descendants to situate themselves at the centre of their narrative was praiseworthy and beneficial. However, the way it went about this raises questions. Racial presuppositions were held to be self-evident, projected onto representations of past sub-Saharan civilizations, without considering how those who had created them saw themselves. One need not have precise knowledge of these two movements, which are not the only ones of this kind in the Afro world, to have at least encountered some of its manifestations. These conceptions emerged in Europe and in the United States where racism is the daily bread. Where contempt is commonplace. And in both places, they were formulated by individuals who were cut off from their sub-Saharan roots. The Cameroonian sociologist Jean-Marc Ela emphasized this point with regard to the theorists of Negritude: '[. . .] the characteristics by which [they] define African identity belong to a conceptual heritage transmitted in Western culture. In a sense, the sources of "Negritude" are European.' Ela goes on to describe Negritude as 'a "petit-bourgeois" movement for intellectuals torn between European culture and African tradition; it reveals the plight of elites disconnected from the real African world.'[2]

This stinging critique was not unique. A good number of other sub-Saharan authors denounced this approach. Everyone recalls Wole Soyinka's quip, 'A tiger doesn't proclaim his tigritude, he pounces.' For this English-language sub-Saharan writer, the identity proclamations of Negritude theorists did not make much sense since they did not manifest the identity that they were intent on

---

2 Jean-Marc Ela, *Le Cri de l'homme africain* [The cry of the African man] (Paris: L'Harmattan, 1980), pp. 146–47.

exalting. It would have been more meaningful to actually be, rather than waste energy saying what they thought they were. A counter-discourse is pernicious insofar as it engenders an imprisonment in the coloniality of which it ultimately becomes a component. It is a hollow *marronage*, since it perpetuates the degrading combat with the oppressor. A battle that is fought over and over again, and from which one never emerges victorious.

Attempting to deconstruct or respond to the dominant system amounts to pretending that one can cure it of itself. The hope is to make the stay on the plantation more pleasant, when the point is to leave it, to reach the *quilombo*[3] and build another world. It must be stressed, however, that English-speaking sub-Saharans, who were also colonized, and who produced nothing comparable to Negritude, were not the only ones to criticize it. Many French-speaking sub-Saharans rejected it too, including philosophers Marcien Towa and Stanislas Spero Adotevi, who wrote seminal books in the field.[4] It should also be kept in mind that sub-Saharan autocrats, inspired by Negritude, capitalized on the desire for emancipation of the populations in Africa, instrumentalizing the identity component to divert attention from the equally crucial problems facing them. People were too busy passionately throwing themselves into authenticity, whether they claimed to be rediscovering it or making it out of whole cloth, to hold their current governments

3 In Brazil, *quilombo* is a village founded by people who had themselves broken free from slavery.

4 Marcien Towa, *Léopold Sédar Senghor: Négritude ou servitude* (Yaounde: Editions CLE, 1971). Stanislas Spero Adotevi, *Négritude et négrologues* (Paris: UGE/Plon, 1970; Montreuil: Le Castor Astral, 1998).

accountable. What's more, the latter presented themselves as restoring the traditional conception of power, according to which the words of the chief, his very person, will tolerate no dissent. In other words, for the heads of neocolonial states, dictatorship was a cultural feature. It is worth remembering that Negritude had fierce sub-Saharan adversaries, and that it was in Africa that this conceptual framework was most violently criticized.

Likewise, it is among African Americans that the most vehement oppositions are found to Afrocentricity, and more broadly to cultural nationalism. In *We Can't Go Home Again: An Argument about Afrocentrism*, African American historian Clarence Walker explains his objections to this reading of history.[5] He notably refutes an idealized presentation of African history and the absence of respect for the real life of African Americans in the country they contributed to building. The majority do not question or suppress their Americanness. The fact that the country did not treat them correctly is a different matter: they do not identify with any other and do not think of themselves as a sub-Saharan diaspora in America. Their history is also, perhaps even especially, that of a struggle to belong fully and completely in the nation. During the days of segregation, they fervently sang 'Lift Every Voice and Sing', known as the Black national anthem. It was a transgressive statement, no doubt—since they did not sing 'The Star-Spangled Banner'—but indisputably American. And it was not uncommon in integrationist Black circles to sing nationalist songs such as

---

5 Clarence E. Walker, *We Can't Go Home Again: An Argument about Afrocentrism* (New York: Oxford University Press, 2001).

'America the Beautiful', which was performed by some of the greatest artists of the community, including Ray Charles, Whitney Houston and Aretha Franklin. In the complexity of the real life of African Americans, never was the energy of protest annihilated, never was the critique of the system stifled. As the title of his book makes clear, Clarence Walker denounced the fantasy of going back to Africa for those who had won the right to be at home in the United States and whose struggles were aimed at legitimizing their belonging to this country. When Mary Fields, nicknamed Stagecoach Mary,[6] delivered the mail in the heart of segregated America, this woman, the first Black employee of the postal service in her country, was not dreaming of Africa. Black history in the United States abounds in such personalities, people who felt like Langston Hughes, Harlem Renaissance poet, when he wrote 'Let America be America Again [...] Let America be the dream the dreamers dreamed'.

Not seeing the dream come true tormented them and they, like Langston Hughes in his equally famous poem 'Harlem' ('What happens to a dream deferred?'), predicted the explosion. But for the vast majority, returning to Africa was not a goal. Such is the experience of the African American masses, which Afrocentricity found so unworthy. Even within the radical Nation of Islam movement, where Malcolm X earned his stripes and which advocated separatism, going back to Africa was not on the table. Indeed, the

6 For more, see 'The Life and Legend of Mary Fields', *Women's History Matters*: www.montanawomenshistory.org (last accessed on 24 October 2023).

origin myth that was invented by the Nation of Islam (Elijah Muhammad) had nothing to do with it.

It is nonetheless important to understand what spawned and then fed this type of thinking, which is more widespread than ever. Afrocentricity is all the rage these days in French-speaking sub-Saharan Africa, where people, eager for decolonization to be over and done with, are beginning to lose patience. Negritude is no longer as fiercely questioned by intellectuals there. As Jean-Marc Ela observes, Negritude assimilates the Eurocentric view of Africa. Thus it was actually an adopted form of Western thought. It operated by a reversal of the stigma, in the way that an insult is owned in the hope of diffusing its destructive power. This deactivation is never effective, since it has no impact on the oppressor whose worldview remains unaltered. A more worthwhile approach would be to invent a new language whose terms are not fraught from the outset.

Negritude does precisely the opposite by defining itself with a word corrupted by history. A word flung at those who were to be cast out from the human species. A word that, for many, was the last spit in the face before they lost their lives in a racist crime. A word that cannot possibly be drawn out of the blood-stained mud in which it was forged. Born in Paris in an intellectual milieu, the idea of Negritude would never have emerged in sub-Saharan Africa where the populations, although colonized, did not suffer at the time from an identity disorder. The writings of the authors of the period were not addressed to sub-Saharans, given that, in their vast majority, the latter had no access to them. It was a period when

French was not widely spoken, no less read. Many people in rural areas of sub-Saharan countries ignored the nationality that had been assigned to them. It was meaningless. For many, the name Africa was unknown. This was how it was until their remains were laid to rest.

Theorists of Negritude were speaking in France and to France. That was where they were published and read. That was where they sought to establish an African presence. The literary quality of the texts is not in question, neither is their consoling function or offensive power. Great authors emerged during that period. Language cannot express the recognition that we, who had the advantage of reading them in school, owe them. We owe them gratitude for having so brilliantly begun the job that falls upon us to introduce our experiences into human consciousness. It was a chance, indeed a privilege, to receive from them the words and representations that shaped our imaginations and continue to enrich us. Their aesthetics forged our writings today. Their thoughts, still all too unfamiliar to a wide segment of our readership, strongly irrigate our thinking, flowing as it does through the underpinnings of our texts. But how many of us were there, in this Africa whose vastness is reduced by maps?

The authors of Negritude remain tutelary figures. As I have often said, Césaire's *Cahier d'un retour au pays natal*,[7] which I discovered at the age of twelve, was my first literary shock. I had never

---

7 Aimé Césaire, *Journal of a Homecoming / Cahier d'un retour au pays natal* (N. Gregson Davis trans.) (Durham, NC: Duke University Press, 2017). Originally published in France in 1939.

read anything like it. I did not understand why my parents did not have the book—or any other written by a sub-Saharan or Afro-descendant author—in an otherwise well-endowed library, and this text prompted me to seek out those writers of whom I had been deprived. Luckily, the school curriculum in Cameroon focused extensively on sub-Saharans or Afro-descendants. But I needed more. Reading them was a necessity, a long-time obsession. Those writers shaped me. But they were only human, sensitive beings influenced by the context in which they moved. Negritude authors adapted to a political framework, without truly conceiving of another. The same could be said of a great number of their contemporaries. They were the colonized in an assimilationist environment, unlike their peers from English colonies who were able to inhabit their identity more serenely. The extent to which the French colonial system, which pretended to make Gauls out of sub-Saharans, was damaging in terms of self-esteem can never be emphasized enough. An entire book on the subject would not suffice to examine how destabilizing and neurosis-generating it was, particularly for those who would become intellectuals.

The most radical artists and theorists did not escape the structural hold that this system had on their minds. Thus Cheikh Anta Diop titled his most famous work *Nations nègres et cultures* (1954), when nowhere in Africa did nations describe themselves as Negro. The most basic mark of respect you can show people is to designate them by the term they use for themselves. This racial definition could not be of any concern to people living in a space populated by melanoderms.[8] It was clearly because the racist view propagated by Europe had been internalized that there was a need to negroize these ancestors whose history and achievements were sufficient in their own right. They were speaking of themselves, not of their ancestors, and to Europe, the sole interlocutor to whom they had to prove not only their humanity but also their greatness. Europe had racialized civilization, and the very idea of civilization. The colonized intellectuals felt the need to answer this racialization in the same terms. They would propagate the racial definition created by imperialist thinking, without ever going to the trouble of returning to sub-Saharan fundamentals as far as self-understanding was concerned. Thus, Diop strove to give present-day relevance to a Black past, to *civilisations nègres*, to borrow a term from the title of another book by him, *Antériorité des civilisations nègres* (1967),

---

8 Far be it from me to contest the assertions of those who translate Kemet (the original name of ancient Egypt) as 'land of Blacks' instead of 'black land' as others do. Who am I? Nonetheless, one wonders what reason there could have been to distinguish oneself from others by skin colour when one does not live all the time in their presence, when everyone in one's immediate surroundings is melanoderm and, especially, when a nation is so powerful that it is the beacon of the world. On this continent where peoples had many names for themselves but not that one, this position ascribed to the ancient Egyptians seems unwarranted. Antiquity was not racialized in the modern sense of the term. No one defined themselves by their complexion. Why would they have been the only ones to do so? Why would the pharaohs, who were living gods, have felt the need to stand up against the rest of humanity and proclaim, 'Here, we are in the homeland of . . . Blacks'? The attitude seems anachronistic, laughable and, especially, alien to sub-Saharan usages, all of which supposedly emanate from Kemet. I find the name *remetou*, which means 'perfect men' in Medu Neter, the language of ancient Egypt, more convincing, all the more since related names are found elsewhere in sub-Saharan Africa.

translated into English as *The African Origin of Civilization* (1974). Cheikh Anta Diop's writings are not to be thrown to the winds. His output is vast and merits study and examination. What is important to keep in mind is that he, like others, was a colonized author crossing swords with the oppressor. This situation certainly impacted his approach.

If Negritude was being written about in Europe, more particularly in France, this was also the case for Diop's research work, which could not have existed without recourse to European sources and which no one in the sub-Saharan countryside was planning to undertake. At the risk of upsetting some, it is worth pointing out that the search for traces of one's past, the need to consult the archives in whatever form, was not a preoccupation in most pre-colonial sub-Saharan societies. Archaeology was not practised there. The relationship to what Mamoussé Diagne[9] qualifies as memorable—what is worth remembering—could be limited to a cosmogonic and genealogical order, to the cult of ancestors, to the memory of glorious events. The relationship to time was different.[10] The point here is to measure the deep-seated upheavals that colonization triggered in the psyche of the sub-Saharan elite, and of the intelligentsia in particular. The colonized who came to Europe—where people live surrounded by the material achievements of

---

9 Mamoussé Diagne, *Critique de la raison orale* [A critique of oral reason] (Paris: Karthala, 2005).

10 Manga Bekombo Priso, *Penser l'Afrique: regards d'un ethnologue dwala* [Thinking about Africa: Views of a Duala ethnologist] (Nanterre cedex: Société d'ethnologie, 2009). The author examines the concept of time in Duala society of Cameroon.

ancestors whose names are featured on plaques and whose busts stand in the centres of squares—could not help but wonder what their ancestors had produced while others were building palaces and cathedrals. It so happened that, having poorly conducted their investigations or having deemed their discoveries of little value, they tried to ennoble the void they found. It is in this vein that we can interpret Césaire's famous cry: 'Hurray for those who have never invented anything / for those who have never explored anything / for those who have never vanquished anything.'[11]

A bogus celebration for the sub-Saharans who were to read this, and for the Afro-descendants whom the poet wanted to connect to the original continent. So it seems that he had not been impressed by the ruins of Great Zimbabwe, or by those of Loropeni that raise questions for which researchers have found no answers. That he knew nothing of the Vay or Meroitic writings. For him, only European technology bore the name of invention. Exploring and vanquishing were bound up in Césaire's mind with the conquering gesture of Europe, wherein could be seen the natural course of human existence when settling in a place and making it inhabitable. Inventing, exploring and vanquishing are what people do to live, without it being ineluctably synonymous with trampling on others of one's kind. Be that as it may, these lines from Césaire, which sub-Saharans recited in school over and over again for decades, demonstrate that it did not suffice to have written that 'For centuries, Europe has force-fed us with lies and bloated us

---

11 Césaire, *Journal of a Homecoming*.

with pestilence'[12] to be truly convinced that this was so. One has to feel powerfully torn between two parts of oneself, between two logics, to lambast the lie and endorse it in the same breath.

As for Afrocentricity, a theory that we owe to the African American professor Molefi Kete Asante, it too emerged in the heart of Westernity and started out as a restoration of the African contribution to the history of humanity. On the basis of the anteriority of human presence on the continent, Afrocentricity undertook a rehabilitation attributing all the merits to Africa. In the first stage of Afrocentricity, the elements that Europe had stolen were what imparted value to the original land. Little attention was paid to the rest of its heritage. Afrocentric essentialism rejects the idea of an Afropean identity. According to this logic, Afro-descendants, wherever they are, must be seen as Africans. They are not granted the right to define themselves, to assert a singular identity, to claim an attachment to a land made prosperous by their ancestors, as slaves or immigrants.

The source of these sensibilities is to be found in the history that racialized sub-Saharans and Afro-descendants and in the place it assigned to them in the world. This spawned the idea of racial solidarity before it was a question of laying down its cultural underpinnings. Identity is firstly race. Through it one recognizes those who have undergone the same oppression and who might share common cultural traits. The feeling of belonging to a Black nation, numerous and present on several continents, made it possible to the potential of collective liberation. Let us recall the world in

12 Césaire, *Journal of a Homecoming.*

which our ancestors lived, even after the transoceanic deportations and colonial slavery:

> No other people in the world suffered as much physical oppression—deportation, slavery, colonization—and negation of the self. In 1918, the Negro civilization, the African culture, the originality of the Black world did not exist. Before speaking of national or social liberation, Negroes have to regain a sense of self-esteem and dignity; the proto-nationalism of these years must necessarily pass by way of the global rehabilitation of the Black world.[13]

The negation mentioned in these lines concerned all areas of private and social life. Science did not take a backseat when it came to contesting the humanity of people of sub-Saharan descent. Philippe Dewitte was speaking here of the time of the Harlem Renaissance (1920), the artistic and political movement that inspired Negritude. Léopold Sédar Senghor was born in 1906, Léon-Gontran Damas in 1912, Aimé Césaire in 1913. Negritude was created in the 1930s by very young men. The independence of African countries was not yet on the table. It would take another thirty years for this to come about, and in a trafficked form. There was, to be sure, an Afro activism in European France in the years before Negritude. Several journals were founded in this context: *Le Messager Dahoméen* (1921), *Les Continents* (1924), *La Voix des*

---

13 Philippe Dewitte, 'Les mouvements nègres en France. Conclusion Générale' [Negro movements in France: General conclusion], *Hommes et Migrations*, *Trajectoire d'un intellectuel engagé, Hommage à Philippe Dewitte* 1257 (September–October 2005): 8–15.

Nègres (1927), *La Dépêche Africaine* (1928), *Le Cri des Nègres* (1931) and *La Revue du Monde Noir* (1932). These often short-lived media outlets wavered between assimilationism, internationalism and pan-Africanism. In them, race and the need for racial solidarity was always a concern, more or less intensely. Nowadays, in the Francophone world where decolonization is incomplete, the preoccupations are not very distant from what they were then. Except that, on the continent, the problems are not posed, broadly speaking, in racial terms.

The pain of dispossession persists, the imbalance of power too and, perhaps, uncertainty as to the possibility of one day reversing this situation. On the part of the members of a group perceived around the world as the dregs of humanity, this fragility is understandable. One can no longer pretend that little is known of sub-Saharan and Afro-descendant cultures. Yet, they rarely become references. Perceptions of the continent and those who are associated with it have not improved. Since racialization focused so much on appearance and on the body, the image that one projects is paramount. This preoccupation can take on a tragic character. Instead of a reappropriation of the self, it often reveals an obsession with the discourse of the other, which is somehow obscurely expected to provide a form of validation.

The importance ascribed to appearance often signals the internalization of the dominant criteria of beauty, even in cases when people profess to being liberated from them. Presenting oneself to the world decked out in finery that is (or is professed to be) sub-Saharan, trying to satisfy European codes of elegance at all costs, especially if one is living in a minority situation, is a way of expressing a discourse. Clothing signifies. That's not new. In multicultural societies, even when people are only heeding their personal tastes, what one wears gives rise to political interpretations. Not always without reason. Let us reiterate the understandable interplay of the personal and the political for members of minority groups. The weight of society's gaze leads to submission or confrontation. Clothing, finery and hairstyles are the most accessible weapons. Ones that reveal the lack of other available tools. Moreover, it is possible that recourse to the ornamental as an instrument of combat misses its target and merely sublimates the strength of an ill-fought adversary.

If I bring up *Black Panther* again, the blockbuster from Marvel Studios, it is not only because it seems to have become the yardstick for understanding an Afro future but also because watching it was a micro-traumatic experience for me. It treated the question of appearance in a way that placed Africa and the West on an equal footing, rather than holding differences and originality in high regard. As was the case, to an extent, with the literary output of Negritude, it was less a matter of being themselves than of letting others know what they thought they were, and, in the case of the movie in particular, of demonstrating that they had pushed to its limit the mastery of the technoscience created by the West. Thereby asserting not so much self-empowerment as the ability to supplant the other after taking over their throne. Thus, borrowings from Africa were relegated to folklore while all manifestations of power

were Western.[14] That this suits African Americans may be understandable, but the sub-Saharan infatuation with it is troubling, as
is the incapacity of intellectuals of the continent to examine the
film in depth. They celebrated *Black Panther* for the opposite of
what it was in reality, that is to say, a work of self-colonializing.
'Self-colonizing involves the total internalization of the foreign
gaze. Third World society understands itself through categories of
the other, rather than through its own [. . .] Dispossessed of the
knowledge of their reality, 'uprooted' from the interior, the members
of Third World societies have one desire only: to identify with
Westerners.'[15]

Given that this internalization of the other's gaze is the main
aesthetic impetus behind *Black Panther*, it is hardly surprising that
any perspective of evolution or elevation outside the Western
paradigm is denied. When T'Challa, having become king, decides
to open his country to the world, it is not to Africa that he turns.
His first and only public declaration is made to the United Nations
which still exists in this Afrofuturist film where the place of sub-
Saharans remains as peripheral as it is today. Audre Lorde's famous
statement, 'The master's tools will never dismantle the master's

14 Anything related to power is foreign to Wakanda, and hence to Africa. The
herb that gives the Black Panther its strength is a plant that has mutated when it
came into contact with a meteorite: its properties are extraterrestrial. As is vibra-
nium, the miraculous mineral that makes the country so powerful. The technology
is utterly Western, in form as in function.

15 Serge Latouche, 'L'échec de l'occidentalisation du monde' [The failure of
Westernization of the world], *Revue Tiers Monde* 25(100), *Le développement en
question* (October–December 1984): 881–92; here, p. 891.

house', has been forgotten once again. The methods of the oppressor are thereby legitimized and Africa is consigned to a desire for Westernization. The architectural references to imperial Africa and the costumes of the characters serve as an ornamental device, nothing more, since the agenda of the film lies elsewhere.

The vibrant defence of Westernization was not the least of the paradoxes in a story set in a country that had never been colonized, and whose population, preserved from European domination, could not have considered itself Black. Let us leave aside the political thrust of this dismaying film; there would be too much to say. We should nonetheless stress the weight of the inferiority complex that led to aberrant aesthetic choices because the point was to show an ultramodern Africa according to accepted standards. With its squeaky-clean silliness, *Black Panther* answered the need that many Afro-descendants have, above all, to be seen, even if this is accompanied by a problematic discourse, since the movie sent them back to Africa to imagine themselves in a position of power. While driving them out of their homes to return them to the sub-Saharan sender and construing Afro-descendance as corrupted by an overly lengthy association with Whiteness,[16] *Black Panther* fulfilled their need for a restoration of and through the image. For the duration of the fiction, the original continent, normally the object of contempt, was in the limelight. There was just enough dust, troubles— outside of Wakanda, in the real Africa—and purportedly ancestral

---

16 Agent Ross comments that Killmonger (note the name) has 'been with us too long' to explain the violence beyond redemption of the young African American. This I quote from memory, as I have not been particularly eager to see the movie a second time.

customs[17] for viewers to remain convinced that it was truly the Motherland. This, more than the story, is what won Negrohood over.

There is good reason to be baffled by the Afrofuturist approach as it is promoted by the African American director Ryan Coogler, who set out to invent the future by denying the past, propel us forward eyes shut to what happened and to what we are a product of, and without formulating any critique of the present-day system. It is in watching the earlier animated TV series *Black Panther* by Marvel Knights Animation, released for online streaming when the film came out,[18] that one can better grasp what informed the studios' project. As cynical and vain as it may seem, some people in the West, whether or not they are of sub-Saharan descent, feel a need to imagine that at least one sub-Saharan territory was not colonized or touched by any Euro-American influence. Not only would this country have escaped the predatory aims of all the Western nations engaged in their enterprise of appropriating the world, but it would also have been the bravery of this nation's warriors that made it possible: 'The Wakandans have a warrior spirit that makes the Vietnamese look like . . . well, the French', one of the characters in the animated series explains to his colleagues gathered in the White House situation room. One can see here how uncomfortable it must be, in the end, to have made all these nations bite the dust. How, in looking at the past, it sometimes

---

17 The annual combat for the Wakanda throne is far from any sub-Saharan practice. Even as a joke, the thing is inconceivable.

18 Marvel Entertainment, 'Marvel Knights Animation: Black Panther, Episode 1' (2018): https://www.youtube.com/watch?v=ry8e5ldzLDQ (last accessed on 8 May 2024).

happens that one wonders if so many deaths and so much destruction on all levels were really worth it.

So one rewrites history; it feels good to invent undefeated, invincible sub-Saharan heroes. The fable is of no use to sub-Saharans. They were colonized—very much so, no doubt about that. In fact, this is precisely to what they owe all the names used to designate them. Their victories are in the future. They will be those of people who have managed to draw the best from their past in order to free themselves from it and invent their new world. More dynamic and more vivid, the animated series was of greater interest than the movie. It provided a critique of Western civilization by the Wakandans. With a cast of other Marvel heroes, including Captain America, Juggernaut and Storm, the series presented itself for what it was: fantasy entertainment. It had a limited impact, however, and seems to have run for one season only.

In *Black Panther* the movie, which set out to tell a story embodied by characters with whom viewers could identify, there was no credible self-invention. Nobody recovering after a brutalizing history, healing their wounds, gaining strength. Nothing but the creation of fantasies with no greater effect on reality than a fix affording the fleeting rush of artificial paradises. The dream participates in emancipation if and only if eyes are opened, if people stand up and move forward. The Afrofuturism of *Black Panther* was at once an escape and an act of submission, for there is nothing more Western than reducing Africa to attire and ancestor worship. The manifest ambition of defeating oppression with an ostentatious show of lip plates and shimmering clothes leaves one somewhat dubious. If the point was to promote the idea that no sub-Saharan modernity rooted in endogenous knowledge and practices could exist, the movie was a resounding success.

The world at large sees Africa and everything to do with it as firstly defined by lack and incapacity. So it is expected from all those who might bring value to this region of the world to advance in life bearing this unique banner. A great many Afro-descendants know this: the racism that they have to face comes from the fact that they are associated with Africa. While waiting for the continent to resemble an immense Wakanda, it must be claimed and proclaimed, if not built. How could it be built when the energy needed to do so is dissipated in vain discourse? And since it constitutes the part of oneself compromised by history, the painful part of oneself, the part that was long shameful for many, allegiance is owed to it alone. It is the failure to respect this exclusivity that has led to Afropea being decried or seeing its significance mutilated by some who profess it. Anyone with a sub-Saharan phenotype, especially if they live in a Northern country, is expected to assert absolute loyalty to sub-Saharan Africa. The paradox is the following: to survive racialization and all its corollaries, it happens that people take hold of them and entrust them with a mission they cannot fulfil. Even overturned, the stigma cannot gain liberating power.

I myself resort to vocabulary forged by racialization. Current practices and the sensibility of people to whom my solidarity could be wanting lead me to say that I am Black. This term has no validity other than political. I know nothing, for instance, about Black feelings, which means that the word does not speak of the being as such. I introduce memorial elements into it out of faithfulness to the memory of the deportees of transoceanic human trafficking, as testimony to my deep-seated affection for Afro-descendant populations whose daily life is marked by race. But I remain convinced of the imperious need to extricate ourselves from this, to come together around other foundations, to reconnect with our face, our truth. These are not to be found in the words of others. We alone can define and expose them. At the dawn of the twenty-first century, the time has come to prepare ourselves to bid farewell to the Black race, to question without complacency the attachment to this category. In saying this, I do not mean to minimize the impact of this racial fiction on the lives of sub-Saharans and Afro-descendants. In France, as elsewhere in the West, racial confinement is the first characteristic of the Afro experience. From this standpoint, it is understandable that race is sometimes conflated with identity, which it has so strongly influenced.

I invite you, however, to consider the fact that, in the rhetoric of the people who have purportedly given it thought, it seems to constitute the key identity referent. There is no question of forgetting that racialization, which negatively constructed colonized alterities, led to marshalling creative, spiritual resources against it, and to strategies, and political activities which recognized both its destructive power and its force as a catalyst for self-recreation. Through opposition to its dehumanizing nature, racialization triggered responses of all kinds, which have in turn produced cultures and ways of living. All these refutations taken together, and the arts of living that took shape through them, form the part of the Black being that escapes the racialist construction, the reifying ambition of slavery and colonialization. What was forged through resistance, through the practices of self-esteem and of affirming and defending human dignity, was not planned and was not supposed to exist. It is to the beauty of the unsuspected that we are drawn when we celebrate our Black peoples and sing the praises of our Black cultures. All of which is understandable. But have these words become ours? Do they belong to us enough for it to be clear to all what they denote when we say them? That *Black* is the inner light that we managed to project outside to counter the night that was meant to bury us? Will the dictionaries ever say what we mean by *Black*? There are plenty of reasons to doubt it, given that our epistemological influence is nonexistent and language being what it is: decolonizable via the addition of a new vocabulary or the broadening of vocables through catachresis, but impossible to de-structure altogether. The unexpected that I've been discussing deserves to be drawn out of the darkness, wrenched out of the dark. That is what was at stake, that was the goal: to be oneself, not what others tried to construct. Therefore, not to be Black.

In the global imagination, powerlessness is the primary characteristic of the Black being, the *blackness*[19] that the French language is not authorized to conceive of. This is one of the reasons, incidentally, that many contemporary sub-Saharans, when they live on the continent outside societies marked by racism (like South Africa or Mauritania) do not think of themselves a priori as Black. As Joseph Ki-Zerbo said, 'It is not because we are Black that we

---

19 In English in the original. [Trans.]

are poor, it is because we are poor that we are Black.'[20] Black then is firstly a way of emphasizing inferiority, which diminishes the possibility of it ever being a healthy identity marker. The insult does not change in nature when it is worn as a badge of royalty, or when concepts supposed to unite sub-Saharans and Afro-descendants are fashioned from it. Historical hindsight shows this to be true and argues in favour of adopting a different language, a vocabulary created by those who desire to speak of themselves. A terminology that repudiates both the constant confrontation between Black and its opposite, and the idea that the memory of those concerned, even their history, starts with racialization. This is not the case for sub-Saharans. It cannot be the case for Afro-descendants who cherish their sub-Saharan filiation. Individuals who are the pride of the continent, those with whom present-day activists identify so that they can feel important and position themselves in a line of free-dom fighters, refused to adhere to racial thinking, even when they recognized the importance for people of sub-Saharan descent to join forces against the racism that plagues them all. Let us cite in this regard from Julius Nyerere's speech to the 1974 Pan-African Congress:

Let us make it quite clear. We oppose racial thinking.

[…]

For although this Congress movement was made necessary by racialism, and was itself originally confined to black people, our particular struggle for dignity has always

---

20 Joseph Ki-Zerbo, Dani Kouyat (dir.), *Identité/Identités pour l'Afrique*, documentary film (Burkina Faso, 2005), 52 mins.

been one aspect of the world wide struggle for human liberation. [...]

For if we react to the continued need to defend our position as black men by regarding ourselves as different from the rest of mankind we shall weaken ourselves, and the racialists of the world will have scored their biggest triumph.[21]

The sub-Saharan spirit managed to resist the racial aberration. The history of the populations of this region of the world did not begin with the colonial conquests. Even after having been colonized and racialized, sub-Saharans have continued to find endogenous spaces of self-definition and legitimation. Among themselves, they do not live according to the categories into which the exterior gaze has tried to fit them. They are, above all, Ewe, Muluba, Bété, etc. These identities preceded the colonial period and have outlived it. The languages spoken south of the Sahara continue to evidence the alien character of the notion of race. The terms mistakenly translated by *Whites* to designate Europeans refer to other aspects than skin colour. These words are always different, in each given language, from those that refer to the colour white.

One of the best known of these terms is *toubab*, commonly used in the countries of Sahel, by people speaking a variety of languages. All hypotheses dissociate this term from the colour white, and the most likely suggests a deformation of the Arabic *toubib*, which means doctor, initially referring to the military medic of the

21 'Julius K. Nyerere's Speech to the Congress', *The Black Scholar* 5(10) (July–August 1974): 16–22.

colonial period. In the Ewe language of Togo, the word for the colour white is *he*, while the European is called *yovol yevu*, which signifies cunning. No doubt they must have noticed some craftiness. In the Duala language of Cameroon, the term for the colour white is *sanga* while the European is referred to as *mukala*, which translates as bird's foot. In Bété, the language of Ivory Coast, Europeans are *gɔmlan*, those who look old. Baoulé, spoken in the same country, regards the European as a *blɔfuɛt*, which means an inhabitant of the land of the dead. Human beings are not designated by the supposed colour of their skin. I invite the good speakers of sub-Saharan languages to undertake this investigation. The result will speak for itself.

As for the term *black* used to define oneself, in the sub-Saharan languages that sometimes employ it, it is a translation of the European designation, and its use is recent. One can readily demonstrate that the practice did not exist in pre-colonial times and that the significations of *black* in many sub-Saharan languages are hardly positive, as is the case in Europe. Here too, obscurity is black. Here too, the colour white symbolizes purity or spiritual elevation. It is hard to see why sub-Saharans should adopt a racial viewpoint that is foreign to them at its origin, does not reflect their view of humanity and traps them in what they themselves see as an obscure space. That others wanted to project their shadows onto them should not influence the course of their lives and the way they read their history. The sovereignty of the continent will only be possible to the extent that one's true being is reclaimed. It is problematic and necessarily detrimental to establish one's dwelling in forms chosen by others to express their contempt, and to satisfy the taxonomy that they set up to consolidate their domination.

For all these reasons, it is commendable that Afropea—the most recent Afro-descendant category, the closest to Africa in both geography and history—has adopted a vision that does away with the poisonous fabulation and sees to it that the stigma, even in its illuminated version, is no longer the primary common denominator. Identity is not in colour but in culture and life experience. Race may not sum up all of life experience in Western societies, but it is, for the time being, inseparable from it. This is a fact. To decolonize them requires first seeing oneself with one's own eyes, not with those of colonialism and racism. This is the way to break free from the racial burden.[22] This particular form of psychological pressure that affects minority groups having to confront racism damages the well-being of individuals who find themselves forced to anticipate the way they will be perceived by the majority gaze. The efforts they make are not noticed, let alone recompensed, and the importance given to the outside gaze diverts the capacity to act from its purpose. Toni Morrison articulated this point well in a speech to Black artists in Portland, Oregon in 1975.[23] She describes racism as a con game, a red flag dangled in front of the bull, a strategy whose purpose is to distract the victims from their real work and divert them from their own power. This is what happens every time one feels

22 Douce Dibondo, 'Qu'est-ce que la charge raciale qui pèse sur les personnes non-blanches?' [What is the racial burden on non-White people?], *Glamour* (7 May 2019).
23 Toni Morrison, 'On Black Artists', Portland State University, 30 May 1975: https://www.are.na/block/3717250 (last accessed on 16 May 2024).

obliged to respond to the slightest verbal aggression, to being ignored or poorly judged, and to show how sensitive one is to it. If the words or acts fall under the purview of the law, it is appropriate to take legal action. If that is not the case and one does not feel the need to change legislation because the matter is not all that serious, then one must concentrate on what is really important. Freeing oneself from the negative gaze of others starts with transforming one's own perspective.

In addition, the question of culture, which is particularly important in structuring identity, deserves to be raised. How would Afropeans of France define their culture? How would they describe it? Is there an identifiable Afropean culture, one that justifies that it be given a name? Does Afropea have a symbolic language capable of conveying its experience and setting it apart? This is not a trivial question when one considers this category as forming a group within a country of deep-seated regionalisms, where all see themselves as having their roots in specific regions that are deemed immemorial. For Afropeans, whose space is also found elsewhere, more in the particularities of experience than in a national territory, what referential figures, what cultural practices, what aesthetics would be apt to characterize this population and motivate the designation?

There is a need to be able to unite around aspects accepted by all, notably concerning referential figures and moments of communion. It is important to lay claim to a heritage of one's own and to highlight it so as to have something to share with others, including with people of sub-Saharan descent. There must also be community institutions worthy of the name, whose function is not confined to fighting against Afrophobia. I will refrain from making any suggestion at all as to how to make all this exist: it is not my role to speak out on this. However, to respond is important. What makes belonging to a new ethnicity such a huge opportunity is that these things are decided and invented as much as they are received. Which involves defining oneself and letting it be known.

There are complaints that the French of only European descent are not always able to differentiate between immigrants and the native-born. It should be said that the conflation of the two is maintained on both sides. There are also complaints that it is easier for sub-Saharans to enter the Afropean literary field because they are capable of approaching it more light-heartedly, having grown up in an environment where their expression was not hamstrung. They are also thought to have an easier time getting their voices heard, in a system that is always playing one against the other and has no desire to open up on its margins. This is not untrue. Having heard this reproach directed against me—in my absence—during a debate between Afropean artists and activists, and articulated in terms similar to arguments against cultural appropriation, I decided to stop writing novels that could be read as Afropean. The irony of the situation is that I had to fight to introduce Afropean characters into the French literary landscape, particularly with my novel *Blues pour Élise*, the publication of which led to a clash, and then a break, with the publishing house. The tetralogy of which *Blues* was the first volume did not see the light of day. I no longer want it to, for this episode in my career takes me back to the violent disagreements with the French publishing house Plon. The participants in the aforementioned discussion were mostly women who were readers of my books. I know how important my writings were for them as for many others. The problem was elsewhere and I could not be indifferent to it. If there is the slightest risk that my voice stifles others, who are more directly and more intimately grappling with the subject, it is imperative that I hear this. It is mainly up to Afropean authors to take charge of their history, to inhabit their country, the entire space that surrounds them, this Europe that is theirs in their very self-definition. Nothing that is human is alien to us, of this I remain convinced, and I do not feel that it is illegitimate for me to tell any story. It is out of solidarity that I step aside. The legendary laziness of French cultural circles makes them quick to choose a person, and one person only, for a given task. As a result, the diversity of points of view is wanting, which only aggravates frustrations.

I have sometimes found what some people post on social media greatly perplexing. There is an obsession with Africa on the part of Afropeans, few of whom have been there, and about which they know exclusively from books and videos on the Web. All this is done with the energy of despair. That of having taken so long to love this continent and no longer be ashamed of it. That of being French-born and experiencing this as something painful. These feelings are rooted in the rejection of a society that has belittled parental cultures. A society to which they belong but in which they are not recognized. The yearning for this recognition interferes with the development of autonomy, which in turn complicates the acceptance of their European belonging.

In her analysis of the identity-based tension among children of migrants and the way in which it hinders subjectivation, turning origin into an impassable hurdle, Alice Cherki explains that it cannot be otherwise in a society that rejects the references to which these children are attached. Not only does this prevent them from breaking away from their origin, but also their very origin turns into the bulwark against anything offensive or destabilizing, trapping them in a firm, unshakable and thus frozen identity.[24] In my opinion, the solution would be to create spaces where people can revere what they wish, support one another and love each other. Groups are like individuals in this respect: self-esteem and self-fulfilment make for healthy encounters with others. The problem is that Afropea aims at a union that is impossible to achieve without an encounter.

Afropeans who try to turn Africa into a fortress where they find refuge from their constant vexations, a lifeline that allows them to escape their painful sense of belonging in Europe, are not exactly expressing their love for Africa. In this case, unlike the children of migrants whom Cherki discusses, the sub-Saharan origin that they tend to overemphasize is a distant one. They do not know it and it was not necessarily what nurtured them most. The fact is, one cannot love what one does not know well, what one has approached only virtually. Africa is utilized to mask the distress and torment

24 Alice Cherki, 'L'identité, royaume de l'illusion' [Identity, realm of illusion], *Lignes* 3(6) (2001): 228–32.

of being an integral part of an oppressive system; after all, these Afropeans invest their energy in it through their work, spend their resources on it, consume according to its prevailing practices, and would be crushed if deprived of even the most basic comfort to which they are accustomed.

The task of transforming society seems daunting to many Afropeans. So they look from afar at this Africa that they desire and fear. This Africa that would gladly do without being the object of fantasies for yet more centuries to come. This Africa that has better things to do than serve as a placebo for the malaise of people, whoever they may be. So any possibility of affirming their presence in France is deferred, because doing so involves owning their bond with the others—meaning, with Whites. That is, with those who are collectively consigned to the status of atavistic tormentors, which makes them undesirable and objectionable, except if they enter the relational space proposed to them with heads bowed. Those who, for their part, get all bent out of shape whenever minority voices express their point of view, who describe any community initiative as separatist as soon as their supremacy seems threatened, and demand that their fellow citizens be satisfied in their subaltern positions. Protest is permissible solely to the French of European descent, since the country and anything said about it are their privileged preserve.

In an environment where everyone is looking to save their skin and where rejection is answered by rejection, it is not easy for Afropea to make itself understood. Instead of an oppositional approach confined to arguing against the Eurocentric discourse of hegemony, Afropea formulates a critique of Westernity so powerful that it can only aim at dismantling Westernity itself. This differs from a primarily oppositional stance because Afropea, as defined by its very name, proposes an utterly new path: one that does not lie either in confrontation or in merely reversing the present situation, enabling the last to become the first, but rather operates within the same framework. Again, in contrast with postures of confrontation or reappropriation that believe that the keys to the future are to be found in an obscured past and regard the intrusion of conqueror-Europe into the historical trajectory of sub-Saharan populations as a demiurgic act, Afropea's approach is one of emancipation. That is to say, Afropea posits the acceptance of a responsibility insofar as the future of peoples is concerned. To call oneself Afropean is to work towards the renewal of the bond, to feel implicated in the destiny of all. Not to deny the past but to have learnt enough from it to understand how important it is today to contribute to inventing what will be. This will not be possible without recognizing what testifies, within the self, to an imperishable relationship with the other. This awareness is what allows Afropea to be written without a hyphen while nevertheless emphasizing the differentiation of terms—the initial separation.

The name Afropea makes visible and imposes the permanence of this relationship, as much as it manifests the desire for the meeting between the parts to result not in fusion but in what emerges from the encounter, what is created from the cross-fertilization between the two. Afropea is the sole Afro-descendant designation that proceeds in this manner. It projects itself into a future that leaves no room for internal rupture or resentfulness. Afropean duality is positively audacious, for it dares the alliance of terms immured by history in a seemingly irrefragable antagonism. This is what makes it a post-Western conception, a fraternal proposition and a demand for inclusion. Laying claim to two great spaces means nurturing both of them, inside and outside oneself, equally. Concretely, neither of the parties can be confined to the private sphere. If they are equal and constitute inseparable terms, they will emerge together, one with the other and within the other.

Another compound noun composed in a similar way appeared in the past and resurfaces from time to time. This is the concept of Eurafrica, which might look like an older relative of Afropea but is not—not by a long shot. It was in the late nineteenth century that the Eurafrican project surfaced. In France, colonialists took hold of it, until the Great War, in view of a rapprochement with Germany. The aim was firstly to set up a European federation in which Germany, which wanted to regain its colonies, would not feel that it had been short-changed. It proved to be ineffective, but the Eurafrican current endured and evolved. For France, the project became an instrument of power, a tool allowing it to ensure its independence vis-à-vis other powers and to reconfigure the modalities of its colonial presence.[25]

---

25 Papa Dramé and Samir Saul, 'Le projet d'Eurafrique en France (1946–1960): quête de puissance ou atavisme colonial?' [The Eurafrique project in France (1946–1960): quest for power or colonial atavism?], *Guerres mondiales et conflits contemporains* 4(216) (2004): 95–114.

Eurafrica participates in a Westernity that knows nothing of fraternity. It is an expression, pure and simple, of a particularly French form of cordial racism, a disconcerting mix of desire and contempt, a need to feel loved by the very people that one abuses. In 2007, in his famous speech in Dakar, then French president Nicolas Sarkozy advocated the emergence of Eurafrica, calling it 'this great common destiny awaiting Europe and Africa'.[26] At the 2015 Convergences World Forum, then French prime minister Dominique de Villepin called for implementing a project of Eurafrican cooperation. This recycling of the old strategy comes at a time when sub-Saharan civil societies, especially the youth, are expressing a demand for sovereignty. It is obvious that a project plainly aimed at not losing Africa is in no way comparable to the ambition of Afropea.

To understand the reasons why Afropea is a de facto non-Western proposition, we must restate what Westernity is. I am using the term to designate the character of conqueror-Europe and its American extensions, which humanity has had to endure since the late fifteenth century.[27] It is a way of being in the world in which relationships with others are founded on violence: invasion, appropriation of resources, reification, even killing, and epistemic hegemony. Westernity is what happened to Europe when it expanded around the world and opted for its own dehumanization.

26 Nicolas Sarkozy, speech given on 26 July 2007 ('Le discours de Dakar de Nicolas Sarkozy', *Le Monde Afrique*, 9 November 2007).

27 Léonora Miano, 'Noire hémoglobine' in *Marianne et le garçon noir* (Paris: Pauvert, 2017).

It is unbridled capitalism, the invention of race and racial hierarchies, the cognitive dissonance that makes it possible to tinker with Christian principles in particular and justify committing the worst atrocities.

Westernity is the fabrication of an illusion that, over the long run, is accepted as reality. There are no Whites before the late fifteenth century. It is in constituting itself and seeking its own validation that Whiteness (a racial construct, not a colour category) negatively projects itself onto the populations it encounters. The invention of race through Whiteness imprisons Europeans too. Although Westernity may at first glance seem to speak of power, nothing in it actually does. Quite the opposite. Brutality is not strength. One has to be in the grips of inner turmoil to surrender so enduringly to one's dark side, give oneself over to it to the point of being defined by one's shadows alone. Westernity is a pathology. The good news is that it is not incurable. Many French people today dream of getting over it. Colonial history is a burden that many wish they did not have to bear. They would like to discover the other side of history. But there is a mountain to climb, and practices and concepts to leave behind.

The will to move on shows itself to be less resolute and falters when material interests or privileges are at stake. In that case, people play dead and certain subjects are avoided. The general public in European France is not interested in foreign affairs. Not even when such affairs invite themselves concretely into contemporary France. A report on the restitution of sub-Saharan artefacts in national museums, commissioned by Emmanuel Macron, was submitted to him at the end of 2018. The report by Felwine Sarr and Bénédicte Savoy, subsequently published in a book, spawned a slew of writings on the subject. Yet, the average French person remained silent. They had nothing to say about whether to return works created by the ancestors of today's sub-Saharans and held in Western museums whose directors are nothing more than receivers of stolen goods. To sidestep the matter, the question of whether sub-Saharan Africa has adequate structures for these works was raised. Aside from the fact that such institutions exist or are being built, is it really necessary to point out that the objects in question were not taken from museums and that Africa has no obligation to use Western methods of conservation and exhibition? When these pieces are demanded—which is not always the case—they must be returned. And without adopting this paternalist attitude that consists in making sure that the savages have understood how to treat their own heritage. Any hesitation in the matter perpetuates the colonial attitude.

It is urgent that we succeed in inhabiting the world differently, and stop regarding one's power as dependent on the degradation, subjugation and impoverishment of others. Nobody claims that this will be an easy task for a France from which the world no longer expects ideas but rather luxury products and gastronomy. A France reduced to a department store for Asian tourists and an open-air museum for educated Americans. Only sub-Saharan Africa still lets it do its song and dance, and pretends it is real. Nobody claims that this transformation will be an easy task in a geopolitical environment governed by rivalries and voracious appetites. The world as it has been constructed by the presence and influence of the West. So lasting has been their imprint that they make the most distant regions of the planet seem familiar. There is not a corner of the planet where cities, in particular, tell a story that the West has not branded with a red-hot iron. Those who have the fortune to travel the world over may wonder what it must be like to observe one's domination over so many places. In all these countries, the West is represented by the very way that it approached them, the traces of its passage being found firstly in the material aspect of things. In technological means, in the form. As for substance, it happens that people resist, albeit barely.

Sub-Saharans did not a priori enter into conflict with what came to them from elsewhere. Curiosity, the ability to discern what is valuable, beautiful or simply useful, the tendency to create mixtures kept them from annihilation. Noting the mutation that has shaped all of us in the Africa of our time does not mean lamenting it and dwelling on a past which will not return and which was not ideal to begin with. When sub-Saharans revolted, it was not against foreign culture, but against the Westernity that threatens identities, including those of its propagators. Do we not hear them worry about a possible breakdown of identity? The problem does not stem, as they seem to think, from the outside. In this respect and in others, the disintegration is due to an internal process. And what exactly are we speaking of anyway, since some people in France conflate their ancestral culture with its corruption by Westernity? 'Is the West a culture, like the ones that it destroys? By its size and lack of clear boundaries, Western civilization is not a culture comparable to the primitive societies of ethnologists or the local cultures of sociologists. The West is the result of an extraordinary explosion of thousands of cultures.'[28]

This fragmentation is also what conqueror-Europe propagated. Not a culture as such, but a killing machine, necessarily self-destructive, its engine being the submission of the living, the domination over matter, and its only goal being profit. The triumph of the West over matter does not suffer challenge and leads us to question the lamentations of their nationalists who fear that the world established everywhere by their ancestors is disappearing. The much-decried globalization is another name for planetary Westernization. Wailing over one's own hegemony seems to be another face of narcissism, demonstrating a willingness to dominate but not to pay the price. Even though it remains moderate on the cultural level. Whereas the Western imprint is visible wherever one goes, the opposite is not as true. The presence of people from elsewhere has not altered the structure of European cities or the behaviours that one is expected to adopt there. What testimonies of the relationship would France accept to see expressed on its soil? That is the question that Afropea raises, and immediately answers.

The imperative of cultural assimilation, which goes beyond mastering and respecting social codes to requiring a relinquishment that turns individuals into empty vessels which France can fill, is experienced nowadays as one aggression too many. For ostracized minorities, whose affiliation with the nation continues to be contested since their members are said to be French in strictly

28 Latouche, 'L'échec de l'occidentalisation du monde', p. 886.

administrative terms, the original culture of one's forebears, even when it is not well known or cobbled together, becomes the fortress into which they retreat for protection against a hostile environment. Which explains the sad spectacle of so much misguided activism on social networks. For long years, minorities avoided emphasizing differences and putting forward foreign affiliations. Their desire was to be treated like other citizens and to see the promises of the country's motto fulfilled. Kenan Malik, who compares the French, English and German situations in this respect, notes that it was the authorities of these countries that opted for multicultural policies based on difference:

> The claim that minority communities have demanded that their cultural differences be publicly recognized and affirmed is, then, historically false. That demand has emerged only recently. [. . .] Minority communities did not force politicians to introduce multicultural policies. Rather, the desire to celebrate one's cultural identity has itself, in part at least, been shaped by the implementation of multicultural policies.[29]

Refusing to prioritize a total social and ethnic mix and constantly reminding people of their foreign origins have given rise to a situation that is hard to face. Here is a simple case to illustrate the problem that always crops up in France when it is a question of citizens whose presence is associated with the colonial past. The March for Equality and Against Racism, thus named by its organizers in a

29 Kenan Malik, *Multiculturalism and Its Discontents* (London: Seagull Books, 2013), p. 43.

clear statement of their aims, was also called the March of the Beurs, 'Beur' being slang for Arab. It was not the marchers who chose to make ethnic this turning point in French social life. That generation of French citizens who were considered non-conforming but who sought to embrace their country in the 1980s were not concerned with intersectionality or cultural appropriation. They were protesting against racism and inequality. Their complaint was that they were not perceived as French when that is what they were and how they felt in the depths of their being. Their movement was an act of faith in the country and, especially, a declaration of love. Nothing similar has happened since, and it is unlikely that it will happen again on such a scale. Hanifa Taguelmint, one of the people interviewed in a documentary aired on French TV some years back,[30] put it this way: 'We offered ourselves to France and it didn't want us.' The country's response was to develop a festive form of antiracism, more moralistic than political, in which the definition of racism was given an emotional character. Racism was, above all, the affair of a few individuals who were wrong in not loving others. It was not an overtly political problem, with a long history of negative othering, with social structures contaminated by the country's colonialist experience, and the categorical refusal to relinquish privileges to ensure justice for all and keep the promises of the French Republic.

Urban policies in France did not promote organizations purported to represent ethnic groups as was the case in Britain, according to Kenan Malik. Neither did they reconfigure the concept of

30 Jean-Thomas Ceccaldi (dir.), *Français d'origine controlee: Comme les autres?* [French of controlled origin: Like the others?] (2014), 56 minutes.

equality from guaranteeing the same rights to all—regardless of race, ethnic origin, culture or religion—to conferring new rights to some based on these differentiating elements. However, these policies departed from the British method in semantic terms only. The 'older brothers' initiative, for example, made it possible to avoid direct reference to communities, even though that was precisely what was at stake. The idea of local authorities tasking underpaid men to act as mentors and ensure social harmony seems absurd—and indeed it was. They (the same mentors or others, who knows?) were subsequently accused of being pathological machos who tyrannized their sisters. Wasn't this something that should have been considered before launching the programme? Since they possessed no financial clout, what power could they possibly have in a viriarchy? It is common knowledge that women's bodies are often the sole territory accessible to dominated men.

There was also the support given to NGOs whose activities are now criticized. For our purposes, it is interesting to note how responsibility was passed off to communities—both ethnic and social—to avoid dealing with problems, to contain the anger in districts that were hot spots and to keep populations there that should not have been confined among themselves. What can we expect when, in a supposedly advanced country, society sets up living conditions for some groups in which misery keeps company with distress? It was obviously easier to proceed in this fashion. The Sonacotra immigrant residences[31] already grouped workers by

---

31 Tonino Serafini, 'Des foyers créés pour surveiller. La Sonacotra est née en 1956, à l'initiative du ministre de l'Intérieur' [Homes created to watch. Sonacotra was

origin. And in Paris, there were Malian or Senegalese residences in certain districts. This confinement made it possible to locate undesirables and to apply a colonialist treatment when needed, especially through the police. This is how citizens are turned into foreigners, paying lip service to integration while recoiling from inclusion.

The March for Dignity and Against Racism that took place in October 2015 was very different from the earlier march in the 1980s. The question of police brutality was central in both cases, but equality was no longer on the agenda. Rather than seeing the lack of demand for equality as a sign of defeatism, considering this goal as unreachable, it indicates a slight shift in priorities after facing increasing difficulties. In a context where clearly not all lives matter equally, where preserving one's integrity on all levels is the chief concern, asserting one's dignity seems more important. The demand for equality is implicit. Some columnists commented on the immoderate communitarianism evident at the demonstration, which admittedly included slogans such as 'I will not assimilate with colonialists'. Anthropologist Michel Agier argued, on the other hand, that the focus on special-interest demands was in fact a way of fighting for fraternity.[32]

Identity, however it is understood and presented, is today the final anchor that society leaves to a part of its population. In an age

born in 1956, at the initiative of the Minister of the Interior], *Libération* (11 February 2000).

32 Michel Agier, 'Un universalisme en acte' [Universalism in action], *Libération* (11 April 2016).

passionately bent on recycling archaisms, this state of affairs does not concern minorities alone. And, as I have already observed, in this respect, the minority populations cannot be expected to set their sights higher than the majority group. Quite the opposite. At least in order to ward off hostility, they will follow the lead of the designated rights holders, who day in and day out voice identity-related anxieties, which are unacceptable coming from people who continue to impose their culture on so many others through institutions specially tasked for the purpose. It will be hard to go back in time. The starting point for all work and proposals must be the current state of affairs. Responsibility for effecting positive changes in the present situation falls first on the shoulders of the privileged, those in power. Their choices determine the social climate. After decades of problem avoidance, of pusillanimity vis-à-vis the colonial past and hence of the impossibility of moving on to another historical time, what is needed are acts that clearly indicate what fraternity must be in the French Republic.

For Afropea, which owns both its European roots and its sub-Saharan ties, it seems obvious that a peaceful identification with a country that is still locked in its colonial mindset is inconceivable. Loving one's country does not rhyme with tolerating its misdeeds and approving of its crimes, all the more when one carries within oneself the memory of the victims. Loving one's country means, to the contrary, contributing to making sure that it takes its place in the concert of nations in the most ethical way possible. And it means fighting for this. French anticolonialists had a high ideal for their country. They refused to see it perverted and thought it was capable of proposing something to humanity other than a debasing system. 'My country, right or wrong' was not their motto. They were not in the majority and did not win the battle, as decolonization was still to come. But they made sure that France did not lose its soul completely, and continued to hope that, once it reached the age of reason, it could become that great country with equality of rights and fraternity as its creed.

Afropea says that the hour of maturity has come, that it is time for France to come into its own. The choice is in its hands: that of legitimating all the children of the nation and writing the next chapter in the relationship's history, one that records the effectiveness of decolonization. Afropea expresses the need for a transformation, for a way out of Westernity. Not only must justice be done and injustice be repaired insofar as possible, but the postures of domination must be abandoned in order to usher in a more equitable era. It is impossible to submit to injunctions to accept without questioning the substance of the historical legacy, to pay the inherited debts without blinking an eye, especially when you count among the creditors. It is impossible to revere figures who illustrated themselves in enterprises of conquest and enslavement. Instead of seeing this refusal to embrace the agents of conquest as a condemnation of France and Europe for their colonial past, and a call to repentance, it ought to be understood as an opportunity. By its sensibility, Afropea offers France a chance to revise its approach to notions of power, heroism and prestige. They will no longer be applied to the agents of discovery, to the builders of empires, to colonial officers, to all the individuals whose posterity stands atop piles of corpses.

It will no longer be a question of honouring those who were best at crushing, at methodically plundering, at massacring without blinking an eye, those whose venality engendered cruelty. The world we are aspiring to requires this change. That everyone agrees on this point is the first form of reparation for crimes of such an extreme nature that absolute compensation is inconceivable. Without being subjected to any pressure (where would it come from?), French parliament adopted the 2001 Taubira Law recognizing the transoceanic deportations and colonial slavery as crimes against humanity. The members of the French National Assembly were fully aware that crimes against humanity are imprescriptible, which would justify that the nation symbolically sanctions the criminals. They are no longer of this world, but the consequences of their deeds are still being felt. And those who would exonerate their ancestors, on the grounds that they were not among the powerful in those days, should ask themselves three simple questions: (1) What did these ancestors with clean hands do? (2) Did they consume colonial products (coffee, sugar, tea, tobacco, cotton, etc.)? (3) Did their country profit from the crime? No need to pursue this line of questioning in order to grasp the moral responsibility and the need for condemnations and reparations. France is a post-slavery society through and through—a characteristic that is not limited to the former colonies. People there worked for mainland France where so-called slave-trade products were manufactured, where deportation ships were built, where crews were hired and where traders became rich. The transoceanic deportations and colonial slavery being state crimes, it is firstly to the state that the demands are to be addressed. To the state that compensated slave-holding plantation owners and not the enslaved or their descendants.

When the French Republic put an end to the monarchy, it did not abolish historical continuity. The revolutionaries profaned the tombs of French kings, going back to Clovis I. In several days, they destroyed century-old monuments and melted down the metal to manufacture weapons. They soon regretted what they had done. They reopened the mass grave, recovered what bits and pieces of cadavers they could.[33] Because history cannot be obliterated without taking its meaning with it. Some people even consider that France, the real France, is what preceded the revolution, and that since then we have been living a dark parenthesis that they would like to see come to a close. The same people are the first to take offence at what they see as the effrontery of descendants of slavery who demand reparations. But if France was itself only when it was engaging in human trafficking and slavery, it is hard to see how these, often Christian, plaintiffs would refuse to publicly repudiate those whose deeds were violations of Christ's message. It is easy to demonstrate this to the diehard right-wingers who think setting up Nativity scenes in the lobbies of town halls is an expression of identity-based re-rooting.

---

33 Radio France, '1793, les exhumations de Saint-Denis ou l'encombrant cadavre de la monarchie' [1793, the exhumations of Saint-Denis or the cumbersome corpse of the monarchy], *France Culture* (15 December 2015): https://bit.ly/-4dLV0sO (last accessed on 18 May 2024).

I was not alone in suggesting that the figure of Jean-Baptiste Colbert no longer be honoured. Not that he should suffer *damnatio memoriae*, that he be struck from memory, but that he should no longer be celebrated in the public arena. And what did I not hear in response? I am willing to try to understand what is so upsetting, but in the end, France has ruled on an aspect of its history and concluded that it is a crime against humanity. The question is not whether Colbert was a racist deep down inside. It suffices that we know that there were French people in his day who were outraged by the practice of slavery, which they saw as *lèse-humanité*, a precursor of crimes against humanity.[34] The poignant statement made by the inhabitants of Champagney in Haute-Saône in their register of grievances in March 1789 is widely known today. That Colbert may have been a great minister of the Sun King does not in any way counterbalance a crime whose nature was never in doubt. Without being anachronistic, progressive minds should, in their analysis of these questions, take the condition and point of view of the oppressed into account. They were human beings. That they lived in times that are past does not override this truth. And France, through the voice of the elected representatives of the people, proclaimed it a crime against humanity. These words, which other former slave-holding countries refrain from uttering, are to its honour but at the same time they compel it.

To submit to the prerequisite of justice. To ask in all serenity what one would be willing to sacrifice in order to placate memories.

---

34 Pierre Serna, 'L'esclavage était bien un crime contre l'humanité' [Slavery was indeed a crime against humanity], *Le Monde* (16 July 2017).

To fraternize with those who came into the world through a gaping wound. The descendants of deported or colonized sub-Saharans are French because their ancestors survived the horror of slavery and colonialist violence. No doubt there would have been a price on my head if I had dared suggest, as I meant to do, that Colbert's figure be replaced everywhere by that of Louis Delgrès. In a France released from the colonialist stranglehold, a consensus could be found around Delgrès. The country would correspond better to the self-image it presents to the world if it chose to pay tribute to this man who led his companions in an insurrection against the reinstitution of slavery and had this to say as he prepared to make the ultimate sacrifice:

To the entire universe,

The last cry of innocence and despair.

It is in these greatest days of a century that will forever be known for the triumph of enlightenment and philosophy that a class of unfortunates that are threatened with annihilation see themselves obliged to raise their voices so posterity will know, once they are gone, their innocence and their sufferings.[35]

Delgrès spoke not of race but of a class of unfortunates. Could he have been more French? How does posterity respond to this man and his companions who died in the name of French ideals? How can it continue to betray them by holding in high esteem Colbert

---

35 Opening words of the proclamation made by Louis Delgrès on 10 May 1802: //www.cnmhe.fr/spip.php?article191 (last accessed on 18 May 2024).

who drafted the Code Noir or Napoleon who re-established slavery? On which side was greatness then and where is it now? Those who are alarmed at the imminent disappearance of France, because it will have been invaded by people from elsewhere and dynamited by their ethnic gregarization, feel an urgency in writing, reading and speaking about the country's history without taking into consideration the experiences of its minorities. They think that is the only way for France to continue being France. The idea is questionable, but let us entertain it. This stance defines France by relying on how it engaged in Westernity. How could any of the French who are not and will never be Westerners subscribe to such a history? How are they supposed to inhabit it?

It is the impossibility with which we are confronted in this respect that drives the Amerindians of French Guiana to suicide,[36] a population that presumably perceives its ancestral territory as occupied. It is also the insanity of this attitude that bolsters the view of a good many Afro-descendants from the French Caribbean that France would never have recognized them as part of it. It is the arrogance of this posture that alienates minority groups in European France, pushing them every day a little more to embrace places elsewhere to which they will never really belong and which, quite honestly, have more pressing issues to deal with than welcoming minorities rejected by France. How, one wonders, should an imperialist history be transmitted today in Cayenne or Pointe-à-Pitre, if

---

36 Yves Gery, Christophe Gruner and Alexandra Mathieu, *Les Abandonnés de la République: Vie et mort des Amérindiens de Guyane française* [The republic's abandoned: Life and death of the Amerindians of French Guiana] (Paris: Albin Michel, 2014).

this history is presented as the whole story and as something that should be glorified? The residents of these non-European areas of France are French because that is what France wanted. And it was not out of a spirit of benevolence. France needs these territories. As a maritime power, it has an interest in staying there. France needed the manpower of the immigrants it brought into the country and who produced offspring.

It is impossible today to envisage a discourse on France that omits these presences and their specificities. The point is not to teach children the history of their ancestors' countries of origin if they were not from France. Such subjects can be touched upon in a general way in early grades and delved into by those who opt for those areas of study in higher education. What is essential is to discuss the particular history that the nation shares with each of its minority groups, which makes them as legitimately French as everyone else. Before reminding them that they have glorious ancestors outside of the country, to tell them, in precise terms, why they are French. It is not because of the existence in the past of kingdoms in Africa. Because Afropea presents itself as a transversal identity, a project seeking fulfilment in both the worlds from which it comes, it encourages France to de-Westernize. France has the particularity of not being exclusively European. Some of its regions belong to other geographic and cultural spaces.[37] It is being invited to recognize its multi-ethnic character, the multiple nature of its identity.

---

37 The archipelago of Saint Pierre and Miquelon is an exception for historical and cultural reasons, more than for its location.

This pluralism is hardly new. Some analyses portray the country as a multinational state, given the diversity of peoples—understood as nations originally having their own language and culture—of which it is an aggregate. France is of course not the only country with such a profile. It is also the case for Spain, England and Switzerland, for instance.[38] In France, regional identities, those of the nations of old, persist as best as they can, given that centralization has often caused languages to disappear. Regional particularisms are regarded as different facets of the common identity, now considered the heritage of all, the wealth of the country. That is a good thing. The French from non-European places should be acknowledged and their nations given their rightful place.

News columnists, editorialists and intellectuals never include these distant regions in their understanding of the country, its history and its culture. Accordingly, they are not speaking of France as it really is and as it has been shaped by its conquests. It is more comfortable for them to overlook the fact that this country is not a hexagon—*l'hexagone* being another name for France, based on the roughly hexagonal shape of its mainland territory—but an archipelago, a scattered territory. It is easier for them to shut their eyes to the places where Caribbean Indians were massacred, where colonial slavery was practised, as was indentured servitude, and where women were sterilized, which was a genocidal practice as it compromised the survival of specific populations. These are some

38 Rubén Torres Martinez, 'L'État-nation, le peuple et ses "droits"', *Cahiers d'études romanes* [online] 35 (2017): https://bit.ly/3V4Qf6w (last accessed on 18 May 2024).

of the traumatic experiences that riddle the memory of minorities. One of the first stages in the country's de-Westernization would involve the inclusion of these remote territories not only in the discourse but also in the concerns of the general public. One cannot take pride in launching rockets from French Guiana and remain deaf to the grievances of the indigenous populations of this region, to cite just one example. European France is completely unaware of territorial claims and of protests against such projects as the Montagne d'Or mining concession. They do not make the news outside the place where they unfold. On the cultural and educational level, too, more substantial consideration of these parts of the country must be guaranteed.

Whereas it is widely acknowledged that the representation of minorities living in European France still needs to be improved in all fields, this does not seem to be a matter of concern to anyone when it comes to more remote populations. And yet, like other French people, they should have the privilege of seeing their features chosen to embody the country, internally and externally. Abroad, only the highly educated know that there are indigenous peoples of South America in France, descendants of deported sub-Saharans or of indentured Indians. In what way do people in the French Republic fraternize with the Kali'na, the Teko or the Wayana? Can Marianne be depicted with the features of a woman from one of these indigenous peoples? Those of a Kanak woman? Will the Bastille Day parade ever include representatives of Saramaka and Aluku communities? Rather than a military display, the national holiday should be a celebration of all those who compose France, an affirmation of the bonds that unite them, a prefiguration of the new world born from their marriage. Then, at last, we will have witnessed a post-Western manifestation and an upsurge in humanity.

Afropea, which has chosen a cultural rather than a racial profile, beckons us to step into a post-racist world. It is not a matter of denying phenotypical differences or the impact they still have on our individual and collective trajectories. These simply do not determine who we are and we are not defined by the negativity that others project onto us. It is also not a matter of contenting ourselves with the fact that scientists agree that races do not exist. They thought exactly the opposite in the past. This is not about the advent of a post-racial era in which people claim to attribute no significance to race given that it does not exist. For people of sub-Saharan descent, pretending to not see phenotype is tantamount to not seeing at all. It in no way ensures that one would not have imparted meaning to the object of one's gaze if, by chance, one had seen. Saying that one does not see is, above all, affirming that one does not want to know, that one refuses to be disturbed by all that historical mess, by the whole business of the relationship. Let us, of course, not lose sight that the origin of the notion of race is ideological and historical, and that it is rooted in European colonialism and capitalism.[39]

39 Anibal Quijano, '"Race" et colonialité du pouvoir' ['Race' and coloniality of power], *Mouvements* 3(51) (2007): 111–18.

Because the notion of race has been internalized by a majority of people, different strategies are required to combat it. Without arguing for a recognition of biological races, it is important to complexify the discourse. Mindsets do not change from one day to the next. So there is a need to respond to those for whom biological race exists, and not confine ourselves to formulating objections. If races did exist and if this could be demonstrated, it would still not justify establishing a hierarchy or oppression, it would not legitimate the impoverishment of entire populations and their social subordination. This is the direction that discourses must take, towards an abolition of notions of superiority and inferiority based on genetic or phenotypical differences. The problem is not in the existence of biological races—on which social races are founded—but in the use to which this is put. It seems easier to deny their existence than to combat the temptations to which they give rise. All you have to do is listen to present-day French nationalists to realize that the scientific discourse does not hit home; they have their own. Thus they will readily point to screenings for sickle-cell disease in newborns among certain populations to determine the number and corroborate their thesis of the migrant invasion.

Since sickle-cell disease is a blood disorder that does not affect people of only European descent, it is associated with race and offers sufficient confirmation thereof. Racists rely also on IQ tests, as contested as such assessments of human intelligence may be. With racial differences thus confirmed, they express alarm at the mediocre quality of genetic material that, by penetrating into France, is degrading the White race. For there will always be leftists and globalists to imagine that there is no risk in procreating with inferior races. And even to eagerly desire it. Moreover, it is to the excessive presence of people with a lower genetic heritage that the decline of France is attributed. As we can see, if the aim is to get rid of racism, arguing that races do not exist will not do the trick. The nonexistence of races did not prevent a minister of the French Republic from being called a monkey who should return to her jungle, which only goes to show that class does not transcend race as a social and political category.

Opposing Christiane Taubira's policy as the minister of justice did not require animalizing her. Her policy was therefore not the target. The problem was that an Afro-descendant occupied such a position in a White country, as that is how some people think of it, and that, to boot, she was brilliant, cultivated and not willing to bow her head. There are people in France who harbour a fierce hatred of Taubira for having one day stood up in the French Parliament, sporting braids and radiating power and grace, to pronounce the following words:

> We are here to say that if Africa is mired in non-development, this is also because generations of its sons and daughters were torn away from it; that if the economy of Martinique and Guadeloupe are dependent on sugar and on protected markets, if Guiana has so much trouble exploiting its natural resources (its wood and gold, in particular), and if Réunion is forced to engage in trade so far from its neighbours, this is the direct result of the Colonial Pact [...]

We are here to say that the slave trade and slavery were a crime against humanity.[40]

I bring up the hatred that these words triggered towards her because I witnessed it first-hand, the year my debut novel was published. In the company that was publishing my books at the time, there was someone who moved in political circles and who thought it would be useful to introduce me to some people she knew. At a small dinner gathering held in one of the national palaces, I heard remarks made about Taubira that were beyond comprehension. Just about every Black person then in the public eye was severely put down. The most militant were said to have been bought, or even to have willingly sold out. None, however, were subjected to the slew of insults that rained down on Taubira whenever her name came up. I remained impassive, aware that my reactions were being observed to know whether I could be useful and at what price. When I stepped outside, I thought I would keel over from disgust. I already had deep respect and great admiration for this woman. I also felt a certain fondness for her since an afternoon in December 2004 when we had met at an event in support of Haiti.

What Taubira brought to the space in Centre Pompidou, where the 2004 event took place, was an energy full of warmth and life. Amicably making her rounds among the attendees, she came up to me with her hand outstretched, asking where we had met. Right here, in this very moment. My first novel would not be

40 Christiane Taubira, 'La Traite et l'esclavage sont un crime contre l'humanité' [Trafficking and slavery are a crime against humanity], speech delivered at the French National Assembly, 18 February 1999.

published until August 2005. From that ill-fated dinner on, I could not help but love her more. I had glimpsed what she had had to face without complaint. And alone, since solitude is the lot of those who are pioneers, unexpected and unclassifiable. In the early years of my career, in my desire to give her something in turn, I sent my novels to her through the National Assembly's address, with a dedication. Then I stopped doing so, as I was seized by anxiety each time. Had I written too hastily and made a mistake? Did my dedication lack depth? Had my hand trembled so much that it was illegible? What would she think? Too many emotions . . .

Never do I reread the speech she gave on 18 February 1999 without crying in gratitude. Because it was important that those words be spoken. Because she did so in just the right way and with her characteristic eloquence. It was necessary both to describe the crime and to recall the humanity of the victims, what is owed to them, and the inequalities that persist because of this history. But who paid attention to her preamble to this long speech? 'Our aim is not revenge,' she said. Few people in the country, including in circles that consider themselves left-leaning and whose hunting feats cause social networks to tremble from fear, know what this statement means or have dwelt on it. All that was retained from this moment when a woman from South American France came to restore the honour of her country was her call for repentance. And yet the law had been adopted at first reading in the National Assembly in 1998. Unanimously. And the Senate had adopted it at second reading in 2001. It was as if the nation's representatives had woken up from a spell and wondered, horrified, what they had done. Whence the brutality of the insults some years later. Whence the lack, for a long time, of forceful actions on the national level. The little effort made to identify, to fraternize and to deracialize not the past events, which is impossible, but the reading that should be made of them several centuries later.[41]

Nothing has been done so that people recognize themselves in the figure of the victims and that the latter acquire the status of ancestors. Those whose unpaid labour ensured the prosperity of France. Those whose families could be separated from one day to the next. Those who were forbidden to have private lives. Those for whom love was a huge risk. Those who lived, created and loved in spite of all. The people who were reduced to slavery found ways to live despite their condition. Their experience has so much to teach us. But the subject is too divisive. Enough has been done, people think. Too many in France have a hard time understanding that the crime against humanity calls for adequate measures for those who, without any counterpart in human history, were born out of ineffable violence. To be a descendant of deported sub-Saharans who were then enslaved is to have been constituted by a crime against humanity. It is to have been both born from it and subjected to it. Nothing comparable in scale exists, since we are speaking of

---

41 The Foundation for the Remembrance of Slavery was created in 2019. A memorial to the victims of colonial slavery was planned for the Tuileries Gardens in 2021 but still doesn't exist. These are advances that must be welcomed while remaining vigilant about the capacity of these institutions and structures to promote a discourse addressed to all regardless of origin and to work for future generations keeping in mind the importance of telling them what had happened without leaving them a legacy of pain.

hundreds of millions of people in the Americas and in the Indian Ocean.

Christiane Taubira did not focus attention on what I have just observed. This is worth mentioning so that the radicality of my views is not imputed to her. The woman who was deputy of the first constituency of French Guiana at the time was not asking her fellow citizens to continually flagellate themselves to show how crushed with regret they felt. She was calling on them to demonstrate a spirit of responsibility. To render justice, to appease and to fraternize. Of the three terms in France's motto, fraternity is the one that cannot be legislated. Even if we posit a form of French Republican fraternity, implementing it would require a movement towards and a capacity to recognize oneself in the other. If it is indeed a question of France being a nation.

Removing the word race from the Constitution was an attempt to clear one's conscience, and to do so at little cost since the task of fostering fraternity was not tackled. Then it was deemed appropriate to propose stripping bi-nationals of their French nationality in case of wrongdoing, and in this way their misdeeds were attributed to this foreign ancestry that causes them to be racialized individuals within French society. All the silences and the avoidance strategies worked only to contribute to the rot, leading to this point of no return that had some proclaiming loud and clear, 'I will not assimilate with colonialists'. So here we are, smack in the middle of this deliquescence that many are describing as the decline of France. It is primarily the result of a refusal to consider all its human components as integral to it, all the presences without which there will be not only a collapse but also a plunge straight to the abyss. It is this push to the shadow to which Afropea will not resign itself.

In the French case, Afropea does more than claim its attachment to what comes to it from both continents. It aspires to unite European France with the parts of the country marked by other sensibilities, other cultures and other geographies, both physical and intimate. To acknowledge that an encounter actually took place between populations requires more than gorging oneself on chocolates or dressing up as a Black on carnival days. What is expected as a first step is that France accept the changes that have been brought about in it as a result of the relationship and that it facilitate their free expression, notably on the cultural plane. The French political class, which proclaims its Eurafrican aims *urbi et orbi*, would do well to recognize the multiplicity of French Afro-descendance as one of the constituent elements of its self-definition, if it has any desire for Africa to trust in its good faith.

Recognizing the value of the children born out of the relationship with Africa is indispensable if France is going to pretend to legitimacy in addressing this continent. This is particularly important at this time, when there are sub-Saharan protest movements with names like 'France, Get Out' and when Françafrique[42] is being put on 'trial' in several countries on the continent. So one must hasten to tell it like it is. To teach French youth that they have ancestors of sub-Saharan descent, not because the human species was born on the African continent but because Africa entered French

---

42 The term designates the neocolonial relations of France with its former colonies in sub-Saharan Africa.

history, in its very flesh, several centuries ago. Hard to see why France, after choosing for itself Gallic ancestors who were not ancestors to all and then imposing them on the colonized, now turns around and refuses to recognize its sub-Saharan ancestry. That would be much less artificial. And since the idea of greatness will have been revised, there should be no further difficulty in recognizing themselves, collectively, as having enslaved forebears in the former colonies. Alarmed at the narrowing of French identity and its lack of audacity in opening up and reinventing itself, Pascal Bruckner, an intellectual of renown, proposed the following: 'We can always construct another genealogy; let us seek out ancestors who are honorable rather than wretched. We need to celebrate heroes instead of scoundrels, righteous persons, not traitors, and remain loyal to what is best in us.'[43]

We can only second that motion and say that it is a warped gaze that prevents people from seeing the best of themselves in the enslaved. At least in part. The wretchedness that Bruckner evokes concerns the moral, not material situation of individuals. In this respect, what reproach can be made against the enslaved? Every time they rose up against oppression, it was also the humanity of their tormenters that they were trying to safeguard. To stand up against violence and injustice is to refuse not only one's own degradation but also that of the criminals who destroy themselves through their deeds. And that is heroic. If the experience of people who had the status of slaves remains largely ignored in France and

---

43 Pascal Bruckner, *The Tyranny of Guilt: An Essay on Western Masochism* (Steven Rendall trans.) (Princeton, NJ: Princeton University Press, 2010), p. 219.

elsewhere—including in Africa where the servile condition persists in a variety of forms—that is because human societies generally understand power as synonymous with domination.

From this standpoint, the status of slave is the epitome of the fallen and the vulnerable to whom the worst has happened: being captured, deported, dispossessed of their identity, deprived of freedom and reduced to material indigence. No one wants to identify with such a figure, to claim filiation to it, unless there is no choice. And even then, Afro-descendants would rather identify with an imperial Africa and declare, 'We come from kings and queens', who were themselves often slavers. Because it is more comfortable to identify with the powerful, even if they are not very honourable. The power with which one wants to be associated is not only the power to guard against evil. It is even primarily that of doing evil and having often demonstrated an aptitude for it. This is why it is a fortress in which people take refuge. It is one of the universal perversions of the human race, one that explains why those who master the art of winning without being right continue to impose their law. This expression of power has often found allies and has long attracted emulators.

But this way of looking at things is no longer in line with societies in which the experience of a common history differed based on one's geographic distance, ethnic profile and political condition—for example, that of the colonized. Neither is this approach in harmony with popular expectations. At a time when the verticality and brutality of power are increasingly contested, when the virile order that has prevailed until now is beginning to be reshaped,

when voices once reduced to silence are being heard, the life experiences of the enslaved must be rediscovered. And this can be done
without painting a pretty picture of reality. In these times, when
once-silenced words are being spoken, we can at last tell the whole
story and reveal the nobility of lives perceived as fallen. They were
lives of labour and of a struggle against oppression that took on
various forms, in private and in public spheres. They were lives of
self-invention in places meant for debasement and even annihilation. Lives of suffering, but also of resistance and resilience. Lives
that managed to foil projects that set out to dehumanize them and
create identities, cultures without which we could not describe our
world. If that is the face of defeat and degradation, then there is
no lack of greatness in it.

Those French people who are looking for the way to create an
alternative, non-oppressive society could claim their affiliation with
the maroon ancestors who ran away from plantations and created
other social models. The history of the capture, deportation and
enslavement that produced the Black condition is and will remain
the story of a cataclysm for the victims: whether they stayed on
sub-Saharan soil and had to face the impossible mourning over
those who were torn from them, or lost their lives in the depths of
the ocean during the Middle Passage, or landed in plantations that
would see the birth of generations of humans deprived of the most
basic rights. And yet the people who came out of this crime against
humanity are not known for their resentment, still less for their
desire for revenge. This exists only in small groups and it is
not incomprehensible. But even in these cases, rarely do we find

individuals inhabited by murderous impulses or driven to concoct terrorist plots.

The cultures that emerged from the transoceanic deportations are striking in their uniqueness and the great beauty of their most widely known aspects. France swoons more than most over the cultures of others, without wondering about its lack of interest in its own. It is a fact that the same sub-Saharan sensibilities mingling with those of European nations gave birth to blues and jazz here, ska and reggae there, and son cubano or salsa elsewhere. The African contribution was always of high quality. In France, it gave rise to genres of music that have been little appreciated in the European part of the country. French Antillean music (biguine, waltz and mazurka) is never played on the main stations of Radio France, not even during lengthy strikes when the interminable replacement programmes of music may include unknown artists. The same is true in all areas of artistic creation. This explains why Spike Lee was invited to be jury president at Cannes: there simply is no French equivalent, no Afropean directors who have devoted themselves to showing the experiences of their community. And this is not about to change. Ultimately, what the French cannot stomach about its Afro-descendants is that they are so very French, and therefore they present a reflection that is both unbearable and too much of a likeness. This forces them to come to terms with it, to assume all of themselves, to confront France's history of violence and racism, the failings of the country in this respect.

In France, more than anywhere else, it should be possible to identify with the humanity of people and their oppressed condition, rather than with their race. In France, more than anywhere else, the values embodied by the enslaved should prevail over their physical appearance. In France, more than anywhere else, one should be able to see a Black couple on TV and recognize them, above all, as lovers like any others. For the time being, this seems unimaginable. I would like to share a personal experience that bears witness to this impossibility. Approached by a TV producer who described herself as 'enthusiastic, moved and truly very affected' by an urban short story of mine, I wrote a narrative that was intended to be brought to the screen. The project was found to be very interesting, but the two main characters were of sub-Saharan descent and I was asked to make the man White. He was the one who was more socially well-established. Clearly the attributes of power, even a modest degree of power (he was simply a free-lance accountant) had to be related to Whiteness. Whereas American movies invented the 'magical Negro', a character whose role was to save the White hero or help draw attention to the initiatives and goodness of the White character, the French film industry presents only the 'White saviour', who also figures in American cinema. Their vocation is to enlighten and save the Black person from themselves.

One of the most emblematic examples of this is the TV movie *Fatou la Malienne* (shown on France 2 in 2001), in which the protagonist, victim of a forced marriage, is sequestered and raped for six days straight, until Gaëlle, her White friend, rescues her from the barbaric clan that had sworn to destroy her, encourages her to press charges and then takes her to Brittany to recover. Fatou's friend is not French first and foremost; after all, both the young women are French, even though Fatous is denied this status by the very title of the movie—Fatou the Malian. Gaëlle is White and unsparing in her judgements on the relationship of minorities with their non-European aspect. The film, inspired by a real-life crime, caused considerable damage, not because of the situations it described but because of the solutions that were found and the way in which a community was stigmatized. It would have been different if criticism of objectionable practices had come from the inside, rather than being made by the figure of the White saviour. Adapting a newsworthy story for the screen involves writing for one's time. In a society that is inegalitarian in terms of representation, pointing an accusing finger at the weak and denying their capacity for reform is not to the creator's honour.

I refused to transform my male character into a White saviour, stupefied at being told that the majority public in France today would not see themselves in the couple I had imagined. We are speaking about a country that is turned towards the world and whose movie theatres regularly show original language, subtitled versions of foreign, even very foreign, films. This was the France I thought I knew. This appalling anecdote confirms the hypocrisy of a segment of society on racial questions. The two women who joined forces that day to win me over were the producer who had commissioned the story and someone in an important position in programming of that public TV station. Their problem had nothing to do with the economic precarity of the female character, and with the fact that my story was reproducing old schemas in that respect. No, the Black woman was in her place. It was good to leave her there. But having a White man accompany her climb up the social ladder—which she was beginning to do by her own efforts—and give her his heart would have been so much more meaningful. Luckily, the communitarian argument was not made in this case, as it often is, because two Blacks appearing in public of their own accord is clearly an ethnic gang on the march to do away with the French Republic. Evidently, one must have chosen to associate them for one's own interests, which often run counter to theirs.

Afropean faces are increasingly found in ads. When a couple is shown, one of the two is necessarily of only European descent. But contrary to what one might think, these images are less about advocating multiracial couples than about asserting a concept of integration and even assimilation. Let us put it bluntly: to be a full-fledged member of French society, you have to turn your back on the group from which you come and act as if you are a self-made person. Loving a Black person when you are also Black is considered not only communitarian but also downright racist. A few years back, a strongly disappointed reader approached me at the Paris Book Fair. She had come there specifically to let me know the gist of her thinking after reading *Blues pour Élise*, which had particularly shocked her. In this novel that portrays Afropeans with their families and their loves, only one of the four couples is mixed. And that was racist. It made this reader of mine tremble, physically. How could I!

I held myself back from asking the woman what we, we others, should think every time we saw or read love stories about only White people. Should we nonetheless take into consideration the human experience of the characters, project ourselves into it? Which is what we do. Continuously. Without asking ourselves questions. Even when their lifestyle and culture are different from ours. People who react like this reader are not particularly stupid or bad. Their attitude evidences systemic racism, the kind of racism that silently irrigates social structures. It is not always spectacular and has no need to be so, since it is rooted in old representations, transmitted across the ages, which people unwittingly receive and pass on. Because the plot of a novel is set in France, romantic couples have to include characters who are clearly identified as French, that is, White. Any narrative that does not do so rejects the French, does not desire them, refuses to make love to them. It is the core self-perception that is the problem here. This way of seeing oneself that prevents people from recognizing themselves in their fellow human beings.

A certain form of French arrogance hides an unacknowledged uneasiness, a deep lack of love for oneself. This makes loving others a challenge. These others exist only to validate one's greatness, of which one is not as sure as one would have others think. The uneasiness at being oneself, widespread in France in a variety of guises, makes us wonder how the sub-Saharans could have been subjugated by the French. The violence is there too. Confronted with this pettiness, we cannot help but ask ourselves about the state of the societies that could be colonized by France. If, as the saying goes, the apple does not fall far from the tree, then French people of only European descent cannot be utterly different from their forebears, at least insofar as self-perception is concerned. It was among the colonized that an internal upheaval was produced, fabricating Africans and Blacks where they did not exist beforehand, and providing them with countries, nationalities and official languages. It was among the colonized that a gap, not to say a rift, was created.

A very accessible novel, written for my daughter who was going on sixteen, *Blues pour Élise* speaks of ordinary situations: family, friendship, couples. Could anything be more universal? Yet, here was this woman who woke up, got dressed, went out, paid for a ticket, waited in line, sought me out in the aisles of the book fair, waited for the right moment . . . Westernity is an affliction of unsuspected severity. And if I correctly understood her reproaches, by recognizing our humanity in others when reading these books and watching these films, we are actually being rejected and do not know it. We are consenting to the racism that is directed against us. That is what one could conclude from this and it would not be entirely false. Racism is not only a matter of feeling and morality; it is also and primarily a question of power. The power to prevent you from finding a place to live or a job, to make sure you are not seen or heard, to speak in your place, to subject you to undue identity checks, and so on. Racism has the means to obstruct self-fulfilment, to silence, to erase. It is a weapon of social and psychological destruction.

For Whites and Blacks to be equally accused of racism, and for this accusation to make any sense in present-day French society, there must be a capacity for Mutual Assured Destruction. This is not the case. The resentment that this triggers among minority groups, the acts of rejection that result, the need to seek support among their own, in their own communities cannot be termed racism. That Afro-descendant racists and essentialists exist on French soil changes nothing: they do not have the power to destroy the majority group, whose least fortunate members still enjoy the privilege of uncontested national affiliation, the certainty that they will not be deprived of employment or housing because of their colour, the ease to circulate in public space without arousing suspicion, and the confidence to enter a world created by ancestors whose history is valued. The list is not exhaustive. Generally speaking, those who have this comfort do not notice it and do not measure its importance. Since capitalism indiscriminately produces contingents of the exploited everywhere, people quickly forget that the structure of certain societies is racist, and that, for this reason, the ferocity of capitalism within these societies is compounded by the violence of racism. It is double jeopardy for some. Racism is not xenophobia, which is equally condemnable and present in all human societies since time out of mind. The two words exist for good reason.

Afropea is post-Western because, even though it may be European, it refuses to condone violence towards others, to accept that exploiting, poisoning, expropriating and killing others is needed to maintain a certain standard of living. The very fact that the other is included in its name evinces its opposition to everything that defines the West. This has nothing to do with the old traditions of European populations, with customs that go back to the time when Europe had not yet embarked on the path of Westernity. We do not owe to the so-called Western system the cheeses of the Jura, already manufactured in the thirteenth century, or the charcuterie of Berry, inherited from the Gauls who were already supplying them to Rome by the fifth century. There is nothing in Westernity that proceeds from the creation of a heritage and an attachment to it. Just the opposite. Westernity is bent on trafficking traditional products, adulterating them for commercial purposes. Neither the immigrants nor their descendants, who are the targets of so many complaints, take part in this plundering. In France, interest in heritage readily kowtows to venality. Everything is for sale, provided the price is right.

Capitalism turns everything into commodities. In societies governed by it, it is impossible to survive if you have nothing to sell. Things are more or less subtle, and it is possible to become a commodity oneself. What is shocking in transactions related to prostitution is the very crude way in which they reveal the condition of the majority in a capitalist environment. A good dose of blindness is needed to continue to put one foot before the other day after day. It is also important to remain self-centred, to disregard the fact that all should enjoy the rights one claims for oneself. Witness, for instance, how the demand that petrol be less costly demonstrates a lack of concern for the consequences on the populations of oil-producing countries.

Other products have become so indispensable that how they are acquired is of no importance, as long as there is no shortage. Westernity is a kind of stylized, symbolic cannibalism: it is on human lives that one feasts without much emotion since they are rendered invisible. And when they are not, distance or the fact that they have been lodged in a negative alterity for so long prevents identification, solidarity and concern for justice. These types of behaviour are alien to Afropea. Grassroots political engagement, when it will have become a reality, will lead Europe to a definitive emergence from Westernity. Afropea manifests the presence of the South in the North—two poles that constitute political categories. I agree here wholeheartedly with Boaventura de Sousa Santos for whom the South is not a geographic concept but a metaphor for the suffering caused in the world by capitalism and colonialism. The South also represents the opposition to these phenomena. As such, it exists in the North, through the outsiders, the marginalized, the voices reduced to silence.[44]

With this South in Europe making itself heard, it will ultimately be impossible to make decisions without taking into account the impact on distant populations, all the more when resources are being procured from them. Belonging as it does to both worlds, Afropea favours neither Europe nor Africa. The latter has been invested by a North that, affiliated with its imperialist creator, invites Africa to perpetuate the imperialist work and profits from the fruits of its complicity. Integral to the Afropean perspective is an attempt to correct European hegemony, which may give the impression of abasement to those who would like to maintain it. Afropea aspires to establish a new balance. Present-day Europe still dominates; Afropea cannot do so. By fully taking part in the policies of its country, Afropea regenerates and transforms them. By penetrating European identities that suffer from having been

---

44 Boaventura de Sousa Santos, 'Épistémologies du Sud' [Epistemologies of the South], *Études rurales* 187 (2011): 21–50.

abandoned to Westernity, Afropea offers a future that is richer, healthier and more ethical.

> Identity is not a cage but a point of departure that allows us to add onto the past, to turn it in a different direction. It has always to be reconstructed, and a people, unless it buries itself in its own mausoleum, has to be able to break with its customs, trample on them in order to recharge its batteries.[45]

These lines were not written with Afropea in mind, no doubt because the author, Pascal Bruckner, was unaware of its rejuvenating potential. Yet they support and justify the Afropean perspective by identifying the stunting that can result from a cloistered view of identity. Indeed, France is being called upon to undertake a reconstruction. This starts by accepting a change in identity that allows minority presences to manifest themselves fully. The point is not to work towards the disappearance of heritage, a deplorable outcome that Westernity accomplishes all too well. In terms of culture and identity, it is a matter not of subtracting but of adding and of concretely enhancing the relationship and its consequences.

There is only one remedy for the historically fraught relationship that still exists between Africa and Europe, and this involves a profound reinvention of both spaces. Because, if Afropea is a categorical refusal of Westernity, it is also a call to reshape Africanity. By this term, I am not referring to sub-Saharan identities as such, even if it is possible to posit that they were Africanized. Africanity

---

45 Bruckner, *The Tyranny of Guilt*, p. 187.

is a Western construct. It is what Westernity accomplished in the sub-Saharan space, the trouble that it sowed in the minds, the epistemicides through which indigenous forms of knowledge were denied. Westernity is the dark side of Europe, its sinister power. Only new energy, participating both in Europe and in the space it disdains the most on Earth, will be able to chart a healthy course. To achieve this, Afropea cannot confine itself to refusing Europe's ethical morass, in the hope that this will suffice to improve sub-Saharan conditions. For if Africanity is produced by Westernity, its awareness of itself as a pathology is not strong, which makes detoxification more complicated.

Re-founding Africanity

The idea that Africanity is the result of the fortunately incomplete Westernization of the sub-Saharan space is no doubt disturbing for many. The terms Africa and African themselves are rarely questioned, in an environment where, for historical and factual reasons, only a small minority of the population engages in introspection. Sub-Saharan scholars are highly productive, and have been for a long time. But their work, which is confined to academic circles, has had a limited reach. And even within this intellectual elite, the question is seldom tackled, as if the terms Africa and African participated in an organic process, internal to the continent. Yet, a brief history of the use of these words reveals that their meanings, for those who created them, were not always what we now imagine. Consider the word African, for instance. Until the Second World War, it designated either the European living on the African continent or the native from its northern part.[1]

---

1 Christian Poiret, 'Les processus d'ethnicisation et de raci(ali)sation dans la France contemporaine: Africains, Ultramarins et "Noirs"' [The processes of ethnicization and racialization in contemporary France: Africans, Ultramarines and 'Blacks'], *Revue européenne des migrations internationales* [online] 27(1) (2011); available at: https://bit.ly/3znNAwp (last accessed on 20 May 2024).

Only later did the word take on the meaning with which we are familiar. It would answer the need to distinguish sub-Saharans from people from the Antilles, when the two groups were found on France's European territory. The semantics also evolved to avoid recourse to racial language. Be that as it may, the term African, at its origin, had nothing to do with those who today take pride in this name without having actually owned it. May I refer back to my own reading of these two phenomena:

> A gulf separates [...] assimilation and appropriation. The former, inasmuch as it is an involuntary, unthought ingestion, does not have the value of the latter, which is, for its part, the actualization of a power.
>
> [...] To illustrate this proposition more clearly, we shall say, for example, that the colonized assimilated elements from imperialist cultures without actually appropriating them.[2]

It would not have escaped notice if such appropriation had indeed occurred, if Africa had ceased designating the imperialist ambition of some parties or the prolonged suffering of others, especially in our day, as far as the latter is concerned. Sub-Saharans were saved from annihilation by their ability to adapt and thanks to their cultures, which, battered though they have been, possess resources that kept them from sinking. Those whose being in the world accepts a constant negotiation with the irrational could not be

---

2 Léonora Miano, 'De quoi Afrique est-elle le nom?' [What is Africa named after?] in Achile Mbembé and Felwine Sarr (eds), *Écrire l'Afrique-Monde* (Ateliers de la pensée 2016) (Paris: Philippe Rey / Jimsaan, 2017), pp. 99–115.

totally defeated by the colonialist madness. Sub-Saharans relent-
lessly confronted colonial oppression, to the point that the names
of martyrs echo in an endless litany throughout this region of the
world. When they were not fighters, they offered their resistance
creatively, through mixture and syncretism. Yet, in the eyes of the
world, Africa does not evince any of this. Africa does not evince
spiritual marooning. Africa does not evince luminous melancholy,
the strength to rebuild human dignity on what has become quick-
sand. Africa does not evince the concrete struggle, and the lives
risked and lost. Africa does not evince the bare hands of humanity,
the miraculous weapons of ordinary people confronting the violence of predators.

Africa does not evince the prohibition against hatred and the
ability to distinguish the brother from the criminal: the former come
to learn and find themselves, the latter come only to take and
foment their own downfall. Africa does not evince how much the
mere fact of existing, living, loving and creating there, in the heart
of the morass of dispossession and relentless hardships, testifies to
greatness. Africa does not evince the fact that heroism, the only kind
that counts, has the face of those who were intended to remain
powerless but who wrested joy from misery, the joy of being alive.
Of those whose laughter is modesty and elegance. Those who flit
across the ages while so many populations plod through time at the
cost of unspeakable bloodshed. Africa, at this point, can evince
nothing of us. And the reason Africa can evince nothing of the
people from this space is that it is essentially articulated from the
outside—including by sub-Saharans—or in terms of the relationship that others have with this elsewhere. Africa is not spoken of

from within and for itself in the first place. Sub-Saharans inhabit this name only superficially. It does not know them any more than they master its discourse. For the word itself frames a story, a narrative whose images are impressed on the listener's mind the moment the first syllables are pronounced.

The symbolic meaning of the words Africa and African, which are part of the everyday life of sub-Saharan populations and define them in the eyes of the world, are not in the hands of the people who are most directly concerned. The attention paid to the name, to what it says, to what it projects in the space and especially to the vocation it imposes, is of capital importance in sub-Saharan cultures. Names bear individuals as much as the other way around. Without advocating the idea of absolute determinism, since names change as individuals do through their choices and experiences, they are nonetheless a starting point, one of the most important cards in the deck we are dealt at birth. Beyond these considerations, it can safely be said that name and identity are synonymous, that to know who you are involves knowing your name, that your name situates you and can influence the perception of others. This is because names, even more than appearance, contain something and tell a story. What is there in the name Africa and in the Africanity that is its manifestation?

Some people, who are rarely mentioned when such subjects are brought up, answered the question very early through their own trajectory. Their migratory adventure, which took them from Europe to Africa where they settled, led to their rebirth as a new people. They called themselves the Africans, for that is literally the meaning of Afrikaner, the name they adopted, and that no one to this day has challenged. Since Africa is a European fabrication, what reason could anyone have to deny the Dutch migrants settling on the continent the right to call themselves Africans? Afrikaners speak a language that is no longer entirely that of their ancestors: Afrikaans, the one and only language of the continent to identify itself not so much as African but as *the* African language. That is what Afrikaans means. And here too, rarely is this ignominy mentioned. This is because we know, at bottom, what Africa is, and what Africanity can be, the most resplendent illustration of which is provided by Afrikaner history, with the institution of apartheid and the later creation of the town of Orania, an exclusively White enclave on a continent that, one wonders why, continues to be described as dark. Hasn't the arrival in this space of this population and others dissipated the darkness once and for all?

Africanity is a Western fabrication; it could hardly be otherwise. As is Africa itself, as we know it today. Like the racial designation that was saddled on sub-Saharans from the time of the European conquests, the name Africa is foreign to pre-colonial sub-Saharan thinking. Our ancestors were not Africans. Not a single sub-Saharan deported to the Americas who set foot on the soil of the New World thought of himself as an African or even a Black man. And it is absurd to pretend that 'enslaved Africans united in their Blackness to mutiny'[3] because it was surely not united under a racial banner that the captured individuals, packed

---

3 Kehinde Andrews, *Back to Black: Retelling Black Radicalism for the 21st Century* (London: Zed Books, 2018), p. 169.

into deportation ships, lent support to one another and joined forces against their tormentors. The slavers may well have claimed to see in them nothing but Blacks, but they knew they were humans. And that is what guided their actions. The humans that they were also originated in societies that experienced the domination of the strong over the weak. When we read the stories of the deported told by the likes of Ottobah Cugoano[4] or Olaudah Equiano,[5] and we find racial or African designations in them, this is because the authors, captured at a young age, had assimilated foreign concepts into their original culture. Furthermore, they were writing for a European public, hoping to convince them to fight for the abolition of the transatlantic deportation and colonial slavery. Challenging the vocabulary itself could not have been a priority to them. They knew perfectly well where they came from and what the people of their native land called themselves.

Closer to us, many of the inhabitants of the region called Africa, even after having been colonized, were not aware that foreigners had taken it upon themselves to name their land, and that a change in their identity would result from this. They continued to define themselves as they had always done, in reference to ancestral affiliations. In point of fact, within their communities, the African designation remains secondary, or nonexistent. It is a mask,

---

4 Ottobah Cugoano, *Thoughts and Sentiments on the Evil and Wicked Traffic of the Slavery and Commerce of the Human Species* (London, 1787): https://bit.ly/-3Kcg6Dq (last accessed on 20 May 2024).

5 Olaudah Equiano, *The Interesting Narrative of the Life of Olaudah Equiano, Or Gustavus Vassa, The African* (London, 1789): https://bit.ly/4dS1RB1 (last accessed on 20 May 2024).

a name taken on for the outside. What one truly is can only be known among one's own. These old identities maintain their validity within the nation-states carved out by colonization, even though the recent formations have also become part of one's identity. Because time has passed and people have come into the world in these countries, each of which has its own history, they are attached to them. Africanity does not reside in the love of one's country. To understand what it is and what it will continue to be as long as the exogenous appellation is not invested with a project proper to those most directly concerned, we must keep in mind that it is part and parcel of what descended upon the populations of this continent when others decided to come and do what they pleased.

The 'Africa' project was not conceived for those who are known to the world by the name Africans. Which is why, having named them without their consent, as parents name their newborns, they were not invited to the table to discuss the division of the continent. It was among themselves that the European powers decreed which area would go to which country. It was among themselves that they decided on toponyms to apply to the entities that were distributed. The anticolonial battles did not suffice to ensure that Africa, once restored to its populations, would be seen everywhere and by everyone as the property of its inhabitants. And was it indeed restored to them? In areas formerly administered by France, a system to maintain domination was set up, with the help of local minions. Elsewhere, even without resorting to such mechanisms, former colonial powers contrived to make sure that sub-Saharans were barely tenants on their own land. In divvying up the sub-Saharan space, they forced the populations of this region of the world into an arrangement meant to benefit the West alone. Jean-François Zorn makes the following observation in his reflections on the relationship between the abolition of slavery and the colonization of Africa: 'A single condition would have made it possible not to reproduce the domination: that once abolition was proclaimed and guaranteed, Europe would leave the African continent. [...] By restoring to man as merchandise the condition of man as merchant, Europeans integrated the African into the global market which they continue to control.'[6]

It was a European coalition that worked towards containing sub-Saharans in an environment that was detrimental to them, without leaving them the possibility of building up their defences. Françafrique is understandably criticized, given the criminal character of an enterprise whose seeds were already contained in the plots against the sub-Saharan rulers who refused to take part in the transatlantic deportation. Even then, they did not hesitate to have kings deposed, replaced and, if necessary, assassinated. France's colonial history in Africa is much longer than it may seem. In Dakar on 26 August 1958, as he embarked on a tour of Africa to propose the Franco-African Community, Charles de Gaulle confirmed this in his own way in his incensed remarks directed against sign bearers demanding independence: 'I hail Dakar and Senegal, for three hundred years linked to France and vice versa.'[7] It was

6 Zorn, 'L'étrange destin de l'abolition de l'esclavage', p. 57.
7 Charles de Gaulle, speech given in Dakar, 25 August 1958: https://bit.ly/-44QXfqQ (last accessed on 20 May 2024).

quite some time ago and it was already a lengthy period—three hundred years of quasi-Françafrique that the French knew nothing about. Ever since, Dakar speeches have been repeated again and again.

Nevertheless, one cannot impute the difficulties of the entire continent to the turpitudes of greedy France. To do so is to credit it with considerable influence at a time when all we hear from it are lamentations. French-speaking sub-Saharans tend to think that the grass is greener on the other side, but even a cursory knowledge of the situation in the countries of the continent would readily reveal the mistake. Generally speaking, some problems persist in all countries where the basic needs of the inhabitants are not met. This situation is one of the constituent components of Africanity, an attitude that consists in submitting to the lethal politics imposed by the funding bodies. Their directives cannot be opposed by countries in isolation, and yet Africanity is a poison that prevents sub-Saharans from joining forces in their fight for sovereignty.

If Africa is the name given by conqueror-Europe for its project in our lands, Africanity is what resulted from these acts. The confrontation with a foreign system governing many aspects of life, having to assimilate it quickly and under duress, the assassination, pure and simple, of sub-Saharan leaders who sought a different path could not help but provoke inner turmoil. As resilient, curious and inventive as sub-Saharans may be, as godly, if we are to believe melanin sanctifiers, they had no chance to reflect upon the model of civilization that might suit them. From the time of the trans-oceanic deportations until the era of colonial neoliberalism, their lives were a succession of battles. A transformation did indeed occur, but what did it make of the self and what destiny is to be given to this new being? These are the questions that sub-Saharans have to answer in order to reinvent Africanity. Their space has been invaded since the late fifteenth century and it remains under influence.

Present-day Africanity masks the truths that 'Africa' passes over in silence. It is this rift in the hollow of which sub-Saharans struggle, between an old world whose contours are fading and a new era into which they must project themselves. The continent's development will not be achieved through Westernization. Like other human groups, sub-Saharans cannot envisage the future without building on what they are and determining among themselves what they want to represent and what they desire to contribute to the human community. Undertaking this work requires shutting out external directives and what Africa signifies from the outside. It requires sub-Saharans keeping company with one another and working closely together. The time has come, not to cut ourselves off from a world of which we are a part, but to make our place in it. To choose it, at long last. The place assigned by others is far from resembling what could be if we went our own way. Africanity today is the relentless and exhausting balancing act to which we are compelled when we follow a path charted by others, all the while knowing where it leads.

This mode of Africanity proceeds from a damaged self-image. It sees itself as a victim and limits history to wounds from the past. When it seeks heroes, they are more likely to be pharaohs rather than the populations of the equatorial forest, for the scope of the former's material accomplishments gives them a thoroughly Western aura of grandeur. When it recalls the opulence of its glory days, it looks to figures such as Mansa Musa of the Malian Empire, focusing on his imposing wealth and not on the retinues of captives that accompanied him on his travels. The builders of empires, to which all human groups have given birth, achieved what they did by the affliction of such vast numbers of people that one wonders how they continue to be the object of reverence. These figures are invoked as a reminder that the last were once the first, that they were the most powerful, the richest and the most envied. This is because the West, as the master of the material, imposes the primacy of having over being, and all one can do is conform or perish. This Africanity, born from the rib of Westernity, affects a young generation of students immersed in Western concepts. It is the continuous and impossible mourning for a golden age, which was supposedly disrupted by the collision with Europe and to which it is urgent to return. This Africanity, forged in the deafening rhetoric of a world that perceives Africa only through the prism of indigence, is more aware of its losses and its weaknesses than of its formidable strengths.

If this is how it is, it is not because sub-Saharans have a natural propensity to gripe. The situation can be explained by the asymmetric relationship with a West that never left the continent and that took up residence in the minds of many sub-Saharans. The persistence of the sense of being dominated, of having few inner resources and no recourse to the outside, drives some of the population to see themselves as the foreigners do. It is not uncommon to hear sub-Saharans say that they have no friends, not even allies. This is true, since they are surrounded by predators. But the primary enemies, those who weaken the entire fabric of things and open the door to various lurking threats, are inside. The most dangerous enemy, the one that causes the most harm, is invisible. It has to do with self-esteem. What one is able to create around oneself is a reflection of this. The most harmful form of this alienation that impedes the progress of sub-Saharans is manifested by the credit that is still given to Western discourse and to its recommendations.

To change this state of affairs and rediscover one's own way and one's own voice involve turning a deaf ear to injunctions, ignoring warnings and expressions of regret about Africa being behind,[8] and remaining impervious to feigned sentiments of concern that portray the continent as the main problem of humanity. It means revising international agreements that put the populations of Africa at a disadvantage, and not hesitating to withdraw from certain bodies if necessary. This will be possible only by putting an end to each country's isolation, by interacting more with the continent's other populations, creating partnerships and steadily staying the course. The small states created by colonial conquests cannot withstand the onslaughts from abroad. But pan-African formations could. They would not have to be built on the lines of race or on some supposed fraternity of identity among all in the sub-Saharan space. That

---

8 See Felwine Sarr, *Afrotopia* (Drew S. Burk and Sarah Jones-Boardman trans) (Minneapolis: University of Minnesota Press, 2016).

type of emotional and racialist pan-Africanism, condemned by its incapacity to take sub-Saharan realities into account, will remain a fiction for a long time to come. What might have a chance of thriving will have to be built on the clearly understood interests of the populations and informed by an understanding of the magnitude of the task of getting a multiplicity of singular cultures in the vastest human space on the planet to converse with each other. Only by appreciating the full extent of their differences will it be possible for them to mutually enrich one another. This will not be accomplished in a day. It will take audacity, courage and determination.

Afropea—whose very name precludes such pitfalls as the mythification of Africa, an addiction to resentment and an identity malaise—has the potential to project itself into the possibilities of the continent. It is on its territory, in Europe, that it recasts Africanity in a way that manifests the sub-Saharan facet of its identity. Indeed, whereas sub-Saharans have a duty to forge the content of their Africanity, to impart meaning and direction to it, it is in the space that is still the matrix of Westernity that Afropea strives to bring its different aspects to life. Accomplishing this requires exposing the sub-Saharan sensibility of the new Europe. It is a matter of drawing nourishment from this sensibility so as to transform society rather than restricting it to a protest function, of breathing life into the non-European dimension of Afropea and integrating it uninhibitedly in its space of reference. Since Afropeans are at home in Europe, there is no reason for them to relegate an essential part of themselves to the private sphere, especially since it is beneficial to society.

How does France, determined as it is to strengthen its presence in Africa, plan to demonstrate on its own soil the profound transformations brought about by this devouring passion? Afropea is the answer. For, even though it is now time to pursue the relationship in a healthier way, the imbalance must still be corrected on all levels. In this respect, the cultural and epistemological fields are all-important, not only to reveal postcolonial Europe to itself but also to begin the process of reparation for the symbolic violence exercised on the colonized populations. The Afropean approach is a critique of present-day Africanity insofar as it implements practices that should have been initiated in the sub-Saharan space. This is made possible in the European context which, in spite of its hostility, has the advantage of physically distancing Afropea from the harsh everyday life of a great many sub-Saharans. This re-founding is also underpinned by the necessity for Afropea to abolish the asymmetry within itself, which still immobilizes the relationship between the two components of its identity. Its need to stand on two solid poles invites it not so much to deny the obvious concerning Africa as not to regard Africa's current difficulties as an irrevocable sentence.

Afropea can reconnect with extant ancient forms of sub-Saharan knowledge and restore what has survived the epistemicides and the marginalization of indigenous learning that would have undoubtedly contributed to the emergence of a different model of civilization, another type of modernity. Within the European space in which it is located, Afropea can mobilize various practices drawn from its sub-Saharan heritage and adapt them judiciously. To give an example, this approach would lead to creating different methods of teaching, something that is already being experimented with in France. A case in point is ethnomathematics, a discipline that explores the contributions of the colonized peoples to the field.[9] Ethnomathematics, as a learning method, could exist perfectly well alongside others, the idea being to create a society that values the contribution of all to the advancement of humanity. European science would be enhanced, not amputated by this. In a multi-ethnic environment, these new inclusive disciplines acquire great significance.

In the spiritual realm too, Afropea could turn to sub-Saharan traditions, the positive aspects of which are not lost on it. In an environment that, although secularized, is still governed by thinking and attitudes stemming from the influence of a so-called revealed religion, Afropea is aware of the value of sub-Saharan concepts, which are more in keeping with its inclusive approach. The notion of a revealed religion, for those who subscribe to it, necessarily involves the conviction of knowing truths that have not been communicated to others. When this is accompanied by the obligation to proselytize, as is the case for two of these religions,[10] then the

9 Yann Renoult (high-school teacher in Aubervilliers), 'L'ethnomathématique, un outil de lutte contre les épistémicides' [Ethnomathematics, a tool in the fight against epistemicides], *Les Cahiers de pédagogie radicale* (24 February 2019): https://bit.ly/4bQwsNN (last accessed on 21 May 2024).

10 If I do not here dwell on Islam, it is not because there is any desire on my part to minimize the violence through which it was spread in sub-Saharan Africa, the disdain for and mutilation of sub-Saharan cultures, the genocidal castrations of Arab Muslim human trafficking, the complete absence of discourse on reparations owed to descendants of enslaved sub-Saharans, and the systemic racism rampant

behaviour towards people or groups that do not share this faith is one of domination and conquest. European societies, forged in the wars of religion and shaped to a great extent by the power of the Church, invented enemies for themselves throughout the world, seeing non-Christians, in Africa and elsewhere, as diabolical creatures.

From the time of the transoceanic deportations, the religious argument, which was then an essential component of political life, served as a reason to secure control of both territories and their inhabitants. Since God had revealed himself solely to Christ's disciples, it was to them that he had given the Earth, thereby authorizing them to exercise dominion over all others. Romanus Pontifex, the papal bull issued on 8 January 1455 by Pope Nicholas V, authorized the king of Portugal and his envoys to enslave sub-Saharans. Miscreants by nature, they were offending a Christ they did not know. It was also imperative to take over their lands and the riches they contained or produced. Endowed with this divine right, the Portuguese started settling on the African continent in the fifteenth century and did not leave until four centuries later. The distortion of the Christian message for political and mercantile ends continued through the colonial era.

The general act of the Berlin Conference that partitioned the African continent between colonial powers was ratified in 1885 'in

---

in Arab countries—in the Maghreb in particular—where people of sub-Saharan descent are ostracized to the point of hardly being allowed on football teams. It is rather simply because I am focusing here on France and its history in sub-Saharan Africa.

the name of God Almighty'. So it was God who, having revealed himself to some and not to others, gave permission to mutilate entire peoples, to tear apart communities, to displace them if necessary, to subject them to taxes and forced labour. It was God's power that, embodied in those who claimed to represent him, would violate sanctuaries, destroy or steal sacred objects. God's power would make rivers of blood flow on the benighted continent that was Africa. It is impossible to pretend that you do not recognize a human being when you see one, no matter the person's dress or customs. It is also impossible not to recognize spiritual practices when you see them in action. Yet sub-Saharan spiritualities were denigrated because of the presumed inferiority of those who had created them. Thus Hegel writes: 'In Negro life the characteristic point is the fact that consciousness has not yet attained to the realization of any substantial objective existence—as for example, God, or Law—in which the interest of man's volition is involved and in which he realizes his own being.'[11]

Hence, the sub-Saharans, incapable as they are of abstraction, could not possibly know God, nor really themselves. The arrogance, the cognitive dissonance and the certainty of knowing *the* truth led to the view of a kind of infra-humanity populating sub-Saharan Africa and the relegation of its beliefs to the rank of superstitions. There is as much good sense in literal readings of the Bible as there is in any superstitious system of belief. It is not a matter of advocating the abandonment of the Christian faith by Afropea or in

---

11 G. W. F. Hegel, *The Philosophy of History* (J. Sibree trans.) (New York: Cosimo Classics, 2007), p. 93

sub-Saharan Africa, where, as in the Americas, the oppressed understood the Christian message so well that they sometimes used it to liberate themselves from those who had introduced them to it. In the United States, we find powerful illustrations of this in James Hal Cone's internationally renowned books, *Black Theology and Black Power* (1969), *A Black Theology of Liberation* (1970) or *God of the Oppressed* (1975), which are sometimes studied in France. In sub-Saharan Africa, the theology of liberation, inspired by its South American predecessor, has undergone many developments and modifications. To best address the needs of populations, it built on local cultures. Thus, some thinkers of this current, such as the Cameroonian Jean-Marc Ela, gave a sub-Saharan reading of the Christian message, repudiating a theology of the salvation of souls that looks to Heaven alone and disregards terrestrial realities. They also encouraged seeing the Christ figure in a different light, integrated into sub-Saharan cultures and on par with tutelary ancestors in communities in which it would take hold.[12]

Because Christ was a member of the family, he had a legitimate place in the struggles of sub-Saharans. The thinking of the colonized in the south of the Sahara always wrestled with foreign domination, even where it would have been easier to submit. Sub-Saharans sometimes understood the Christian message better than the propagators of what was called the revealed word. As the ancestral beliefs have not disappeared, the only thing that remains deplorable is the fundamentalism which, among the adherents of the religions of the

---

12 Gabriel Tchonang, 'Brève histoire de la théologie africaine' [Brief history of African theology], *Revue des sciences religieuses* 84(2) (2010): 175–90.

Book, regularly demonstrates its readiness to strike out and destroy anything that does not fit into its worldview. Because the Christian faith was naturalized in the sub-Saharan space, because the populations succeeded in wresting from the initial proposition the forms conducive to the realization of their own projects, there is no reason for Afropea to reject it. The Christian religion was at once a weapon and a consolation. In their work, sub-Saharan theologians have demonstrated that it is possible to appropriate Christianity, not merely assimilate it.

The ability of sub-Saharans to decolonize such imports as language and religion and lodge them at the core of their self-definition without resentment or complexes has no equivalent in Europe. The latter has atrophied from its refusal to own the changes due to the relationship, to experience them in the open and to celebrate having been touched by the other. Only if Europe had allowed itself to be elevated culturally and spiritually by drinking from the sub-Saharan source, thus manifesting a renewed being in the world, could it have been conceivable to regard any of the effects of colonization as positive. Although Europeans often travel to Africa to learn about Bwiti or Voodoo, such initiatives remain marginal and are considered extravagant. On European soil, neither sub-Saharans nor Afro-descendants openly practise their ancestral religions. The first Akan house of worship was founded in the United States in 1967 by and for African Americans. A modest temple of Haitian Voodoo opened in Montreal not so long ago. We have seen nothing of the sort in Europe. In French society, no doubt the world's most secularized, Asian wisdom has taken hold as the most worthwhile alternative to religious practice. Many of those who take this path do so solely in a quest for well-being, demonstrating the Western habit of shopping around in other cultures to liven up their daily lives. For proof of this, just consider the practice of beer yoga invented in Germany, which, as its name indicates, involves drinking beer while doing yoga. Or vice versa, it's hard to tell.

When Afropea takes an interest in sub-Saharan spiritualities, it can turn to those directly related to the tradition of its relatives or be initiated into others. What is essential here is to take the trouble to master the given area, and this cannot be done without knowing the languages. A superficial approach to the question would be senseless and very much like the one mentioned above, wherein Westernity leads to putting the sacred to utilitarian or recreational use. Through sub-Saharan spiritual practices, Afropea finds a fertile relationship with the living that it learns not to hierarchize, a psychological support and, especially, a conceptual framework that embraces humanity as a whole, in all its imperfection. Sub-Saharan religions recognize and punish evil but the notions of sin and heresy are foreign to them. They are non-proselytizing. They do not claim to know the truth or feel compelled to impose it on others, and they cannot be accused of having conducted crusades in the name of the divine. By reconnecting with these forms of spirituality, Afropea also gets back in touch with the feminine faces of the divine power, to these primal and sovereign figures, not necessarily attached to maternity and the home. Here, there is a perspective to share with women the world over who hold dear the metaphysical dimension of existence.

The sub-Saharan societies of the past were not perfect, but like others, they produced beauty and meaning, and many elements that could be an inspiration not only for our time but also for inventing a future in which the worlds that clashed during colonial conquests would at last allow themselves to live in harmony. The difficulties, in this respect, do not reside in the sub-Saharan sensibility, which is readily inclined to mixing and syncretism. Sub-Saharan Africa appreciates additions, and likes abundance which it creates without always being understood. The rigidities are on the side of Westernity. And when some Afro-descendants prove to be averse to embracing or uniting with others, it is, of course, because they are full of pain, because the inequalities that persist in society are not accidental, and also because they have internalized the Western division of humanity. Race—there it is again.

For those who are still at this stage, it is worthwhile to confront the profound thinking of their sub-Saharan ancestors. Furthermore, turning to spiritualities from sub-Saharan Africa would allow Afropea to celebrate its forebears without having to wait for approval from the wider community. As noted in these pages, the existence of Afropea is already centuries old. It has also been argued that sub-Saharans deported to the Americas should be legitimately considered ancestors. Since a portion of sub-Saharan descendants are now European, there is no reason why they should refrain from establishing collective spaces and gatherings to pay tribute to their ancestors, to appeal to them and appease them. Since freedom of worship is guaranteed in France, it is hard to see on what grounds sub-Saharan religions could be disqualified, unless any form of spirituality is prohibited. All Afropea has to do is accept its responsibilities, institute what still remains confined to the private sphere and propose it to whomever is receptive.

The Afropean re-foundation of Africanity also concerns the attitude towards minority sexualities. Present-day sub-Saharan Africa has lost sight of its ancient customs, not only as a result of colonial prohibitions (since the first laws repressing same-sex relations were imposed by the colonizer)[13] but also because of the influence of the so-called revealed religions. Sub-Saharan societies in the past did not always repress intimate relations between people of the same sex. These tended to be codified in environments that considered family, marriage and procreation to be of crucial importance. Relations of this type, which could last throughout life, were not meant to stand in the way of establishing a more conventional family. In some societies, such relations were temporary but not hidden for all that. A case in point is the Azande/Zande society of Central Africa, where an older man who wanted to establish a relationship with a boy had to give the latter's parents a dowry of sorts, as he would have done if marrying a woman. This was a very specific context, but the sexual character of the relationship was clear.[14]

The Azande/Zande society was less tolerant of relations between women, though they did not repress them. These took place

13 Human Rights Watch, 'This Alien Legacy: The Origin of "Sodomy" Laws in British Colonialism' (17 December 2008): https://bit.ly/3yraOkF (last accessed on 21 May 2024).

14 Evans-Pritchard and Edward Evan, 'L'inversion sexuelle chez les Azandé' [Sexual inversion among the Azandé], *Politique africaine* 126(2) (2012): 109–119.

AFROPEA

in polygamous homes where the numerous co-wives did not often share their husband's bed. There is evidence, however, that such relations were not limited to this context. Let us not generalize based on the Zande case. A good many other pre-colonial sub-Saharan societies accepted same-sex relations.[15] Whether it was practices of the court, as in Buganda,[16] the games permitted to adolescents or relations authorized in the secrecy of initiation gatherings, they existed and were not the object of the kind of fierce discrimination that can be observed in Africa today. It is important to refer back to these ancient practices, even if they were unsatisfactory and subject to specific codes. We must remember that we are dealing with a human phenomenon and that it was by no means brought over by Europeans. And because it is a human phenomenon, every society must designate it in its own way. Resorting solely to Western terminology muddies the waters and substantiates a falsehood. Using a European vocabulary to name what is known to all suggests that the practice is European. If all women loving women are defined with reference to Lesbos island, then they will be seen as foreign in their homes. And lives are at stake. Here again, epistemological disobedience is indispensable, in order to find a language of one's own.

During the colonial period, Westerners too had no tolerance for love between people of the same sex. Homosexuality was not

15 Stephen O. Murray and Will Roscoe (eds), *Boy-Wives and Female Husbands: Studies in African Homosexualities* (London: Palgrave Macmillan, 1998).
16 Henri Médard, 'L'homosexualité au Buganda, une acculturation peut en cacher une autre' [Homosexuality in Buganda: One acculturation can hide another], *Hypothèses* 3(1) (2000): 169–74.

decriminalized in France until 1981. And its decriminalization has not protected people from vilification, family break-ups and attacks, which have been on the rise since Taubira's 2013 'marriage for all' bill. Homophobia is common in societies around the world. Homosexuality is regarded as an offence against nature and an attack on the survival of the species, given that love between same-sex couples is sterile in strictly biological terms. In recently colonized countries that are still under Western domination or in Afro-descendant communities, a certain homophobia prevails that verges on delirium, so strong is the sense of being constantly threatened and of bodies being the last remaining territories over which one has control.

The repression and rejection suffered by individuals whose sexuality is deemed non-normative are not a matter of morality as such, except in cases where the revealed religions have made their truth known in this respect. This repression and this rejection reflect, above all, a situation of powerlessness and also, admittedly, come as a reaction to sexual practices among the powerful in some countries of Central Africa (such as Cameroon and Gabon). According to popular belief, in political, business and sports circles, a form of homosexuality is practised that is based on domination and degradation. This is said to be a requisite for gaining access to certain positions or circles. It is said that indulging these passions also involves 'seizing' impoverished youth, the choice of verb here clearly indicating the lack of consent. Another problem has to do with the Western anti-homophobia organizations. To begin with, their activism reinforces the idea of a practice imposed from outside. In addition, the financial assistance they provide to people seen as marginal, and hence secondary, is viewed negatively in countries where everyday life is difficult for everyone.

Also confronted with homophobia based on poorly understood ancestral cultures, Afropea dismisses the falsehoods and recalls the origin of the repression of same-sex relations on the continent. Homophobia is an aberration for sub-Saharan humanism. Many sub-Saharan social practices could thrive in the European context, liberating this environment from its inner darkness, making it a new world. For Afropea, it is a matter of taking the best from the worlds that it has inherited. Its recourse to sub-Saharan knowledge will not damage its European identity. One can very well listen to Bashung in the metro after having honoured one's sub-Saharan ancestors. One can like Racine's plays as much as ancient sub-Saharan epics. Many people on all continents live like this. The Afropean approach entails instituting multiple belongings and giving visibility to the non-European and non-dominant sensibilities that will irrigate the de-Westernized societies of the future.

In analysing the historical relationship as it is taught at school, Afropea would strive to stress the sub-Saharan standpoint, which, having been silenced, is absent from discussions. It needs to be understood in all its complexity, that is to say, approached in a way that does not confine the populations that hold this perspective in a position where they are absolved of all responsibility. This would be tantamount to excluding them from the human community. Having chosen to unite two spaces and their memories, Afropea cannot subscribe to essentialist simplifications. It critiques systems, it does not attack humans and it recognizes the common traits that underpin the universal. These include crime and the abject. If it is true that conqueror-Europe spread its inner darkness throughout the world, its effects became manifest only because other shadows responded to it.

This is not the place for a metaphysical examination of the relationship between peoples, even though the sub-Saharan in me willingly embraces this way of looking at events. More prosaically speaking, let us simply say that, given that Europe is not a deity and faces human entities that are effectively its equals, it can achieve nothing that is not supported by the other party. This is less a matter of approval—in fact, far from it—than of the state in which one finds oneself when the relationship is established. Earlier I raised the question about what it means to have been subjugated by the French, given their discomfort at being themselves. Magnificent civilizations have come into being on all continents. It was never at their apogee that they were defeated, colonized or eradicated.

Weakened populations are the ones susceptible to durable colonial subjugation. Subsequently, alienated populations, having delegated their own power to others, find it turned against themselves. When oppression extends over centuries, it can be seen as a joint production by the oppressor and the oppressed. It is always the latter and the latter alone that puts an end to it. In our day, French influence remains pervasive over a whole swathe of sub-Saharan Africa as a result of local decisions and because there is no common front to counter foreign pressure. No freedom, no liberation is possible without responsibility. Afropea is aware that, on one side as on the other, it has no pure ascendants, untainted by reprehensible behaviour. That does not come down to saying that the blame is to be shared equally between the one who premeditates and perpetrates a crime and the abettor who lends a hand. It means that the darkness in one brings out what resembles it in the other. This is true on the individual and collective scales.

Handing off the entire responsibility for a relationship to the other amounts to relinquishing sovereignty. Asymmetry in relationships results not from the omnipotence of one of the two parties, but from the refusal of the other party to exercise its agency. Being at a distance enables Afropea to see the extent to which present-day Africanity exhibits this reluctance to fully own its power. Sub-Saharan Africa does not lack power, nor is it hindered in its ability to use that power. It controls natural resources needed in Europe and throughout the world. It has the capacity to preserve them, determine the conditions of access to them and ensure that its populations benefit first. The heads of formerly French-controlled sub-Saharan African states behave like a battered wife unable to leave her abusive husband. He offers her trinkets, she pretends to believe the situation is improving, and closes her eyes to the fact that the loans—which will have to be repaid—amount to nothing compared to what is regularly demanded of her. Such conduct testifies to a loss of self-confidence, the unconscious conviction that one is nothing outside the degrading relationship, the fear of taking charge and having to invent one's own destiny. For Francophone sub-Saharan countries, putting an end to this dysfunctional relationship does not mean shutting out the French but, rather, refusing to let institutional and commercial France continue to lay down the law. To extend the abusive-marriage metaphor further, any woman in the thrall of her abuser needs to experience non-toxic relationships, attachments untainted by a long history of domination. Afropea desires the emergence of an Africa that is strong, whose countries are not dependencies of Europe and which does not reproduce abusive relationships with other partners.

It is not in an undifferentiated movement that Afropea embraces the countries of the sub-Saharan space, but, rather, to be nurtured by the best that each has to offer. This pan-African approach is embedded in the name it chose for itself and in the abolition of boundaries that the term presupposes. The thing is only made possible thanks to knowledge acquired through contact with sub-Saharan populations. Africa is not in books or films. Knowing anything of it requires breaking open the piggy bank and going there. This work, like the actualization of Afropea itself, is still in its infancy, but it is clearly underway. The first step in the re-foundation of the Africanity that was manufactured by Westernity resides in this capacity that still eludes the populations of the continent. To know that they have enough inner resources, in every respect, to influence one another in a healthy way, and thereby invent an Africa that can buck the initial schemas. The imperialist programme did not imagine people on the continent coming together and pooling knowledge and practices. Today's nation-states were often created with precisely the opposite objective in mind.

It is a well-known strategy, which consists in taking advantage of existing enmities and keeping them alive, or stirring the embers of resentment and then stoking the flames. Often, colonial state constructions destroyed the structure of existent hierarchies, deliberately bringing together disparate types so that the foreign power could preserve its hegemony and stand as the sole uniting force. Sub-Saharan Africa was colonized by the European nations that initiated the transoceanic deportations. The continent was no longer altogether alien to them, neither were the relationships between populations. The transatlantic deportations sowed terror in the regions concerned, inevitably impacting relations between groups. Some of the disputes that arose at the time persist today.

People are quick to blame the dissensions between sub-Saharans on the ethnic factor, as this is an element that can be readily manipulated by those in power, be they politicians or military chiefs. Research on the ground reveals motives unrelated to ethnicity as such, and conflicts dating back to the time of colonization are among them. Communities are familiar with these old disputes. Fragmentation was at the heart of Europe's African project; it was one of its levers. We are referring here not to the continent's cultural diversity but to organized incompatibility, fractures caused by divvying up the territory between European powers. Very quickly, the sub-Saharans fraternized only through the colonial experience. It is when they leave the continent and become minorities, in European countries, for instance, that sub-Saharans tend to keep company with one another. That is where they have contact with the greatest number of sub-Saharan nationalities and discover cultures with which they were not familiar. Far from their native lands, they live in the same impoverished environment, work in the same miserable jobs, more or less under the table, staying in the shadows to avoid police harassment. Out of nostalgia, they will frequent restaurants and leisure venues that remind them of the countries they left. The permanence of the ostracism will give rise to a visceral attachment to Africa. Their sensitivity in this respect will be all the more intense precisely because they will not be going back for a long time, if ever at all. And so their passion will be tinged with melancholy.

In the country where they live, they will have children steeped in the atmosphere marked by both the country they left behind and other sub-Saharan influences. It is this inherent mix that is found in Afropea and that allows it to elaborate what must emerge on the continent, what can only materialize through exchange and through sharing customs and experiences, but also dreams, for the benefit of all. In this, it restores what Africanity, a fragmentary condition, is not up to creating. It is not a question of advocating some bogus unity between sub-Saharans, but of noting that the change due to colonial history has sown the seeds of a new civilization south of the Sahara. And that, by decolonizing the name Africa, this civilization could confer upon it a content that dovetails with the aspirations of its populations. Afropea intuits an Africa to come, which it prefigures through its cultural practices. As long as it avoids a distressingly superficial *Black Panther* type of mashup, Afropea contributes to preventing a senescence that would endanger sub-Saharan roots.

The European location of Afropea, the fact that it is predominantly composed of descendants of sub-Saharan immigrants, gives it a proximity to the original continent that other branches of Afro-descendance lack. In France, people born of parents from different regions of the continent intermingle and are thus able to weave, from family legacies put into the common loom of daily life, a denser Afro heritage than that of descendants of deported sub-Saharans. The latter did not choose their geographic location or their historical trajectory. Afropea stands apart for the aforementioned reasons. If one avoids essentialists, cultural nationalists and individuals of an unhappy Europeanity who have not understood that Europe will also be what they make of it, it is possible to find people with a serene relationship with Africa. For Afropea, Africa can be at once received from one's ancestors and perpetually recreated. It participates in a dynamic that calms the tensions of being rejected by the country to which one belongs.

Seeing the underside of both sides, speaking both languages, holding firm to a spot where the two are always touching, being a mediating body, it would be hard for Afropea not to dismiss the temptation of victimhood. Given that the imperative of mending the relationship is the condition of its own viability, Afropea cannot content itself with distributing blame. Afropean is a borderline identity, if we understand this word in its old sub-Saharan sense of a place of encounter and exchange rather than separation. Alterity exists but it presents itself as an opportunity. When conflicts surface, their resolution is found in the need to spare both parties from humiliation. Not to pour the other's face on the ground, as sub-Saharans would say. For something will have to be done with this Europe that stifles its soul by refusing even now to recognize what has entered it and will not leave again, what changed it for good when it set out to approach others. To strike a blow or to caress is still to touch. The body cannot rid itself of the memory of contact. The most adamant political stance can do nothing about it: you cannot get away from what is inside you. This is true for one and all.

Afropea is the face of good fortune for Europe at a time when it still dreams of conquests and devalues its identity by attaching it particularly to its colonial action. That this is the case even today is evidenced by the Bordeaux municipality's decision in 2019 to stay the project of paying tribute to Frantz Fanon with a name plaque on a lane in the city. Not a boulevard, not an avenue, not even a street. Just a lane. It is hard to even picture the road in question. The idea sparked such an outcry that then Bordeaux mayor Alain Juppé chose to postpone the plan indefinitely, or at least until historians examined the matter. The protesters, at once vehement and numerous, cited Fanon's participation in Algeria's fight for independence and his incitement to violent acts against the colonizer. And so, when it came to examining values and even principles, France in 2019 mainly recognized itself in the oppressors, probably in their race.

Frantz Fanon was a French citizen who harboured a revolutionary ideal and an aspiration to liberty, which are very much part of the French spirit. By championing the cause of those who would not have had to engage in armed combat if their needs had been heard, he was defending France's honour. The Algerians did not undertake to slaughter the French on the first day of the invasion. When Fanon said, 'For the native, life can only spring up again out of the rotting corpse of the settler'[17]—words that were among those cited as incriminatory in the Bordeaux affair—he was not advocating a massacre. It was a question of toppling a system that was precisely what forced freedom fighters to opt for violence. Is it outrageous to legitimate defensive recourse to violence? Let those ready to answer in the affirmative examine their own history scrupulously before pronouncing judgement. The loyalty of some people to a criminal France, their identification with it alone since they see domination as an expression of power, their hostility to France when it was not imperialist, leads once again to questioning the notion of fraternity as it is understood by the French Republic.

The irony of history is to see Fanon reclaimed by the most fervent French nationalists, who find inspiration in his deeds and his writings for their fight against migratory colonization. Thus Renaud Camus, who first formulated the idea of the Great Replacement, invited his followers to refer to Fanon.[18] Whether to laugh or to cry at the madness of those who pretend to safeguard France and restore its integrity—I do not know. If it is a joke, it is in poor taste indeed to claim that the French are currently undergoing an experience

---

17 Frantz Fanon, *The Wretched of the Earth* (Constance Farrington trans.) (New York: Grove Press, 1963), p. 93.

18 Renaud Camus, 'Je ne vous ferai pas de discours!', speech given in Rungis, France, 2 September 2017, on the occasion of the tenth anniversary of the web journal *Riposte laïque*: https://bit.ly/4ezVD9k (last accessed in 2020; video no longer available).

similar to what the colonized went through. But since some people experience it that way, can one imagine that they expect to see the corpse of the so-called colonizers of today floating on the clear waters of their preserved identity? At any rate, anyone wishing for the end of Westernity and what it engenders surely hopes to see the remains of coloniality decompose. The sooner the better. It is the condition for the birth of different relations between humans. It is the condition for sharing and intermingling in a world where whole regions will soon be uninhabitable. This is not exactly the aspiration of Renaud Camus.

As much as Afropea is an opportunity for Europe, it is also an opportunity for sub-Saharan Africa, which will have in it a sincere and committed ally. Unwilling as it is to accept decisions made by the powerful, its political activism aims at ensuring that its voice is heard and that that it weighs as much as possible in the organizations it joins. The point is not to create an Afropean party, which would be ridiculous and counterproductive. But the lack of an Afropean perspective in the bodies that determine political orientations produces familiar results. The Afropean presence in these circles cannot be limited to adding a touch of colour to family photos, as a token of openness to the downtrodden. The Afropean perspective under discussion is manifested in a discourse, a thinking applied to bringing an end to Westernity. In France, a politicized Afropea would make sure that the promises of the French Republic are kept, for these principles are not contingent and they are as valid at home as abroad. It is unlikely that ties between Africa and Europe will ever be broken. The time has come to rebuild them on new foundations, to annihilate the dominating tendencies of a Europe that no longer knows how to act differently, and to make way for sub-Saharan demands for sovereignty to be met. For these are urgent in francophone Africa where decolonization remains incomplete. In spite of an Africanity that was doctored from the start, despite the doubts, the feeling of living under the wreckage of possibilities shattered even before they had time to ripen, there exist throughout the sub-Saharan space young activists who assert their rights.

These youth, who are not easily fooled, are the voice of an Africa that will soon have sawn through the bars of its cage. Which is why a variety of organizations[19] have rushed to their side, in an attempt to control them through funding, to fill the belly of the protest in order to mollify and to instil in it the fear of periods of famine. It is a known method, tried and tested. Afropea is in a privileged position to enable the decolonization of the two entities of which it is a part. It is in Europe that it will have to play its role, since it belongs to this space and that is where it has a proven capacity to be disruptive. There can be no effective re-foundation of Africanity without the eradication of the Western spirit of domination, unless Africa chooses to withdraw and isolate itself, even temporarily. This is something we cannot hope for. It would be

---

19 I am referring here not to humanitarian action but to structures formed to promote and even guide social transformations. Aid is contingent on adhering to the values of aid giver. Whether these are positive or negative is beside the point. Deviate from the direction they set and the subsidies vanish. This conditional support is a form of control.

detrimental to Afropeans too, since not all sub-Saharan countries accept dual citizenship.

Dreams of a great return from the diaspora to the continent will remain what they are: pipe dreams. Most Afro-descendants will continue to live in their space of reference, even those who will want to maintain much closer ties with Africa. Africa may well be the mother of all, but there is no returning to the womb after having left it. Little does it matter how this came about; it is an immutable law. Leaving, in this case, means being born and raised elsewhere, and having been shaped by it. This does not erase the Afro-descendant character; it specifies it. If Africa alone is granted the status of mother, what would the other lands be? Those where Afro-descendant generations came into the world, which they sowed with their labour, which nourished them in turn, which they marked with their cultural imprint and which impacted them just as much, which were the sites of their loves, where they fought to achieve equality, where their dead—who are also their ancestors— are buried? Often, Africa is the dream land of those who refuse to live in their real countries. It is the kingdom of those who have accepted their illegitimacy to wield the sceptre in Europe or in the Americas, dreaming of a Wakanda whose power would fall from the sky while waiting, arms crossed, for its glory to stream down on them.

Pan-Afropea

The diaspora, in its broadest sense, is increasingly cited as the sixth region of the African continent. This makes more than perfect sense in symbolic, affective and spiritual terms. Politically speaking, this proposition has no reality and will not have so for a long time to come. Sub-Saharan states have yet to achieve sovereignty. Their capacity to work together remains wanting. Considering that Africa is in a situation of having to reinvent itself, it is hard to see how it could permit the integration of diasporas scattered throughout Europe, the Americas and Asia. For, in speaking of the descendants of sub-Saharans around the world, it must be kept in mind that this concerns a good many populations. There is no reason to focus on descendants originating from the transatlantic history. Furthermore, the appeal to the diaspora does not reflect a clear awareness of the wounds that need healing and the political actions needed to enable those who would like to have more concrete ties with Africa to do so. For the time being, the primary hope is to receive investments and benefit from skills. The fact is that the great majority of Afro-descendants are not among the most well-off in the societies to which they belong.

This means that the invitation is not extended to all. Insofar as the populations originating from the transoceanic history are concerned, the prerequisite for any serious attempt to address them would be a due regard for this history. Monuments to the memory of those who lost their lives during the crossing would have to be erected on the coasts from where they departed, along with edifices testifying to the pain of those left behind, to their determination to include in their sub-Saharan communities those who should have been part of them. They lost their lives as sub-Saharans. They did not express their final thoughts or say their last prayers in Creole or in Ebonics. When they revolted on the deportation ships, it was not to reach the other side of the ocean safely but to go back home, whatever their living conditions may have been. When they transgressed the moral and spiritual laws of their people by putting an end to their lives, it was again in the hopes of being reborn on the original land. There is talk today of heritage tourism in many sub-Saharan countries, but the teaching of this heritage leaves much to be desired.

Can those who practise ancestor worship, who consider that the dead are not dead, as Birago Diop says in his famous lines,[1] hope to do right by the living when they have trouble honouring the millions of dead? Knowledge of the world's many Afro-descendant groups remains nonexistent on the continent. What do people in Africa know of the Garifunas or the Gullahs, for instance? And

---

1 Birago Diop, 'Les souffles' [The spirits] in *Leurres et lueurs* (Paris: Présence Africaine, 1960), n.p.; English translation available at: https://bit.ly/3ULmA0A (last accessed on 22 May 2024).

AFROPEA

yet they are part of this diaspora in the broad sense of the term, if
Africa is to continue to be seen as a single womb. This ignorance
confirms the lack of interest on the part of sub-Saharans and the
abusive use of the term diaspora. Colour is not identity and origin
need not be the destination. Those who consigned to silence millions of deportees are hardly likely to fraternize with their descendants. Contempt for servile ancestors is still commonplace on the
continent, between sub-Saharans and vis-à-vis Afro-descendants.
This is sometimes expressed in a brutal manner, for no work has
been done to change mindsets. The living are treated in the same
way as the dead when they are associated with the transoceanic
deportations.

Broadly speaking, in sub-Saharan Africa, the deceased are
regarded as alive. They simply move on a different vibrational plane,
from which they interact with ours. There is no worthy existence
without a powerful relationship with them. This sub-Saharan concept has its particularities, but not a single population neglects the
memory of its dead. While heritage tourism is being set up for
wealthy African Americans, the Atlantic is devouring the coastline,
with erosion gradually making historical sites disappear. In a few
decades, there will be nothing left to visit, since nothing is being
done to counteract this new tragedy. The cart should not be put
before the horse. The task to be accomplished before a meaningful
place can be given to what is not perceived as a diaspora is considerable and internal to the continent.

Is it necessary to again define Africanity as it was fabricated
by Westernity? It is an inner homelessness, a state of being at odds

with oneself in which all the identity proclamations and attachment to customs is but a masquerade. The words are all the shriller in that they are stillborn when unaccompanied by deeds. As regards the relationship to the transoceanic history and the calamitous manner that the subject is treated on the continent, one must bear in mind the fact that sub-Saharan Africa, colonized by slave powers, was subjected to a guilt-producing discourse. The colonizers were the ones who wrote history, who elaborated its official version. Add to this the humiliation of the vanquished and the shame of collaborators, and it is easy to understand what has complicated the tribute to the deceased and masked the figures of resistance fighters and of ordinary people whose lives were destroyed. The part of sub-Saharan history that gave rise to the American diasporas, in particular, is still voiceless and faceless on the continent. Rather than fantasizing about a return that will not take place and that cannot be its project, the Afropean population is committed to building and consolidating its networks on European soil. After all, the prefix Afro in its name is a fixed diasporic marker, meaning that it refers to the point of origin but not to the destination. The members of the group Cash Crew, who posited proximity between Afropeans, were aware of a common condition and, no doubt, of solidarities to be established. The timing for this is right for three reasons.

The first is that Afropeans are more numerous today than they were a few decades ago. The second has to do with the impact of new technologies on connecting, communicating, sharing experiences and pooling resources. The third resides in the political awareness of Afropeans in all the European countries where they are present, and the formulation of common demands. As the European nations concerned are mainly members of the European Union, well-thought-out Afropean synergies could only be beneficial. To borrow Florynce Kennedy's words and address them to Afropeans, 'Don't agonize, organize!' Solutions for the problems that face them will take time to emerge on the national scale. The temptation is great to escape from a more-than-unsatisfactory condition by turning to Black America which has been fighting battles and producing theories for many years. In so doing, practices designed for a specific context are applied to a different one. Its figures and memory are adopted to avoid having to excavate the burial site where Europe has reduced its Afro history to silence. The appeal of Africa is also very strong, for it remains the place of the lineage that must be explored, the place of the spiritual regeneration that must be sought, given that Europe categorically refuses to play this role.

Yet the relationship with Africa can prove to be problematic in many respects. Even for people of recent sub-Saharan filiation who maintain strong ties with their families in Africa, the continent is primarily a place where they go to get a break from racist oppression and the minority condition. People go there as they would head for a few days to the seaside or the mountains for a change of pace. They do not settle there but they like to think that spending time there changes something. For themselves and for those who are there, who will always be there. They are proud to learn that the contributions from abroad have superseded international aid and hence, really, that changes something. Sub-Saharans would not survive without the funds sent by the diaspora. For obviously everyone is standing at attention waiting for someone to feed them.

Sometimes for fun, to liven up my webpages or to get real answers, I propose polls on social media. One of them focused on respondents' interest and personal involvement in pan-Africanism. One woman, a young activist in a very dynamic and highly anti-colonial militant group, said that for her and her ardent comrades in arms, pan-African involvement consisted in sending money to their families living in Africa. I sat there, mouth agape, in front of my computer. All I could do was sympathize in silence with these families. They were no longer loved ones but, rather, instruments of a bogus pan-Africanism. A certain anticoloniality in France is so Western in its outlook and its methods, so appallingly condescending and ignorant that it leaves you speechless. But hey, the priority is not to hurt anyone's feelings. And so no attempt will be made to understand why some activists in European France are capable of tapping into the militant heritage of others but not of developing their own discourse. How did these others do it? Especially the earliest activists who had no model? How did they go about putting themselves at the heart of their experience so that they could speak with their own voice? Is it that cordial racism is so overpowering? Or are they also not plagued by conflicting desires and by a strong Western habitus, despite their claim to the contrary? No one is compelled to understand what pan-Africanism is, to relate to it, to advocate it. Embodying the South in the North does not involve refraining from writing one's own history and becoming in turn an inspiration for others.

The patterns of behaviour that I am questioning are not those of Afropea as I understand it and try to describe it here. These attitudes are rooted in a refusal to embrace all aspects of oneself. The permanent conflict with the European part, this war started again and again and always lost, ends up stifling other affiliations. Because one cannot manage to be from here, one cannot be from anywhere else. It is altogether possible to refuse Westernity, to combat it as Afropea does. It is possible to say no to White supremacy, indicating in the same breath that one has grown up on this European soil and, since that is the case, since that must mean something, that one has taken on the mission of de-Westernizing it. The legitimacy of such an ambition presupposes the following: one has to belong. Without acknowledging that one is intimately bound up with a society and with all those who compose it, it is impossible to hold it accountable and get it to change.

One can indeed refuse to assimilate with colonialists. But what do these words mean? Is there a colonialist ontology? If so, is it possible to assert that it is exclusively associated with Whiteness? Leave aside the fact that this refusal does not seem to have shaken French society, does it propose a strategy for putting an end to Westernity? Racism corrupts France. That is a fact. It will not be overcome by childish invectives and anathemas. The minority condition debilitates. That is obvious. Because solutions seem out of reach, all that remains is a thoroughly understandable but not very effective rage. In this context, the need to put an end to isolation and create collectives of mutual support and assistance is clear. The creation of pan-Afropean networks would strengthen, solidify and broaden the scale of what already exists in the respective countries of Afropeans. By and large, Afropeans do not need visas to travel to the countries of their region. They should use this to their advantage, as it is fully consistent with the designation of their ethnicity.

Because Afropea is European, because it has a centuries-long history in this region of the world, it conceives of pan-Afropeanism as its first and necessary contribution to pan-Africanism. Just as sub-Saharan countries have to create synergies among themselves, so do Afropeans. Before there is any question of demanding that Africa do this or that, that it welcome people in the name of genetic heritage and its potential to become a vast Wakanda, it is important to get organized in Europe. It is indispensable to create a united front against discrimination, develop projects and foster the emergence of Afropean institutions, cultures and aesthetics. A group, a federation of sorts, would be in a position to address sub-Saharan authorities. This movement is what I term pan-Afropea, to designate the profound and permanent solidarities forged in the particularities of Afropeanity. If Africa has duties towards the Afro-descendants originating from the transoceanic deportations, things are not quite the same for those whose ancestors left the continent of their own free will. The latter have to be willing to hear that there were other possibilities, that other sub-Saharan territories could have welcomed those who chose Europe, who decided to give their children to European countries. And rather than lamenting the fact that they were born in this space, rather than trying in vain to rewrite their parents' history, they would do better to find meaning in it.

Among the sub-Saharans who settled in France, some fought French colonialism in their native land. Some see this as a contradiction, the mark of deep-seated alienation, the manifestation of a demonstrable Stockholm syndrome. This was not the case for all. The colonized despised colonial domination and its violence, but they differentiated between that and the culture, and they did not conflate the system with the people. For many, France had not only the face of the colonialist but also that of anticolonialist militants who sincerely espoused their cause, or that of people who were not politically engaged and whose life had simply led them there. Unlike their children and grandchildren born in France, they were not filled with and blinded by resentment. They had given themselves the opportunity to meet other human beings, and that is what must have happened since they did not return to Africa— after all, the continent is big enough that leaving one's country does not necessarily mean going to Europe. And if they sometimes faced racism and were not recognized for their true worth, this did not make them turn around and go back to Africa. They had put down their bags, had made a life for themselves, and remained convinced that it would be an opportunity for their children. Are the Afro-descendants born of this postcolonial immigration responsible for the choices of their ancestors? Almost as much as their fellow citizens who do not share this background, the difference being mainly in the avenues of self-realization offered to them based on their phenotype in Western societies. At bottom, the problem is the same: one does not choose one's family history, but it is impossible to disown it, to pretend that one is not constituted by it.

Therefore it is expected of Afropeans that they choose an Afropean approach, which is the most relevant and the most useful option.

Inasmuch as pan-Afropea is the exchange of experiences and the pooling of resources in order to resolve difficulties that individual nations have been slow to address, it helps to get past resentments arising from the blockages and achieve what matters most. As we know, the question of visibility is crucial to many. But by whom is it most important to be seen? As far as artistic creation in general is concerned, pan-Afropea could obtain the necessary funding. French national productions, even when they tolerate the presence of marginalized bodies, on the screen for example, still scrupulously maintain control of the discourse and the narrative. This gives the false impression of inclusion, when in fact they have ensured that no expression is given to protest, that intimacy is not represented in a satisfactory way, and that complexity is absent from portrayals. And there will never be enough productions of this kind to permit the expression of Afropean plurality, as other minorities must also be suitably represented. This situation has led Afropeans to look for outlets in Africa, to the detriment of local actors. This is not a satisfactory solution either, and it would be hypocritical to pretend not to see the problem. Not only does the Afropean narrative remain absent, but the sub-Saharan discourse is no longer delivered by natives, by the people who live and work on the continent in difficult conditions.

It can never be emphasized enough that colour is not identity. To embody sub-Saharans, being dark-skinned does not suffice. This question, incidentally, comes up regularly on the other side of the

Atlantic, where objections have been made to sub-Saharans playing the parts of African Americans in American productions. Among people of sub-Saharan descent, it is crucial to maintain ethical standards that respect the experience of one and all and ensure that the people primarily concerned are not excluded from the representation of their own history. Whereas there are cries of cultural appropriation in cases when minorities are silenced by representatives of the majority group, there is little concern about minorities sabotaging each other, which is incomprehensible. It is therefore a question of shooting one's own films and finding the means to distribute them, including outside Europe. A collective effort on the European scale would facilitate the task.

As previously noted, there is no Afropean literary corpus in France. It is highly unlikely that widespread illiteracy is the explanation for this state of affairs. After having heard my first publisher tell me that Afropean characters are not universal (but sub-Saharans are), that in fact they do not even exist, and that if I continued to write about them, I would hurt my career as an international author, I confess to a suspicion that the publishing industry does not give due consideration to such texts when they arrive at its door. Because people of sub-Saharan descent are seen as de facto foreigners, the expectation is that what is said about them has to do with these foreign places. They may have spent their whole lives in France, but their literary depictions will always be more favorably received if they spend their holidays in a Sahel village with a grandmother who lives in a hut with no sanitary facilities. It is better still if they went through war as children and fled to France to save their lives, and that the story focuses not on their arrival in metropolitan France but on recollections of the sub-Saharan paradise before the upheaval. Sub-Saharan authors have gained more recognition in France than Afro-descendants. In the latter category, the best represented are the Haitians, from the country that kicked the French out of their island, the country that is not a French department and whose citizens are not French. It is good that everyone's talent is recognized. France is honoured by this openness. However, the silence imposed on European Afro-descendants should be cause for concern. It is also because the Afropean presence is kept quiet, because it cannot be expressed, that it is regarded as not being part of the national story. France knows itself through its literature, which is its mirror and its testament. The silence that must be shattered therefore concerns all French minorities.

Perhaps the fear of rejection is such among Afropean authors in France that they do not even bother to send their manuscripts to publishers, convinced that it is to no avail. Perhaps there is nothing in these works of fiction that merits consideration, paucity being the primary characteristic of these texts. If that were true, serious thought would have to be given to examining why this is the case, why it is that European France has not given birth to a Toni Morrison or even a Zadie Smith, whose pens were soaked in the ink of an experience that reflects that of the country.

France has a hard time keeping company with its margins, and understanding that they inform it about itself and define the contours of its future. Pan-Afropea needs to have a few respected publishing houses, translating the writings of Afropeans and putting them out in their respective countries. Such texts, if they were available, would be of interest to readers of all horizons, in Europe and beyond. Waiting to overcome reservations or be invited to speak up is already a form of renunciation. To oneself. Demonstrating the ability to do without support from established actors is something that inspires desire. It is unfair, since others do not have to put in so much effort. It is unfair, since others are showered with state funding that comes from the pockets of all taxpayers, irrespective of ancestry. It is unfair, but if it were not, there would be no need to fight. The first particularity of Afropea, as a branch of global Afro-descendance, is its existence in a space that has long had the possibility of ignoring it and that is not keen to hear Afropeans articulate its specificities. Changing this situation requires lucidity. It requires knowing where one is starting from and being aware of promoting a project of re-foundation that disrupts the comfort of those who see themselves as entitled.

Westernity will not let itself be destroyed without fighting back, accustomed as it is to parrying blows before they are even delivered. The necessary transformations can only be brought about by implementing appropriate strategies. It is essential not to lose sight of the goal, which is the creation of more inclusive, post-Western societies. Whether it is in France or in the pan-Afropean framework, it is important not to be intimidated by accusations of communitarianism. There are people, always the same, who scream bloody murder to remind us that we are not in the United States, after having proposed to Afropeans nothing other than the example of Black Americans. French minorities have no need to refer to the African American model. They have, right in front of them, a thoroughly French model, the Auvergne network of mutual solidarity that no one finds shocking. And it has proven successful. Afropeans start out more economically disadvantaged, having no real estate or other property transmitted from generation to generation in a perfect endogamy. If one is fortunate enough to belong to one or more communities, the ability to rely on their solidarity is an asset. This is true in France too, as it is a country of deepseated regionalisms where, in spite of Jacobinism, the anchoring in a *terroir*, a specific culture and soil, remains decisive. It is in these *terroirs* that we find the famous French stock that they keep badgering us with. That is where politicians go to acquire legitimacy. France is a country where a prime minister will proclaim that his heart and soul have the taste of salty water to explain why a local mandate in his port city is still indispensable, despite his prominent national position.

For Afropeans, their roots are in the place where they were born and raised. This is also the particular experience of Afrodescendants in Europe. It is important to own this and to learn how to answer calmly, since the aim is to foster fraternity, not separatism. Afropea flourishes better at home and enhances the value of its contributions when it opens its perspectives. Bitterness and frustration end up tainting whatever one has to offer. This must be remedied without waiting for a demonstration of goodwill on the part of those who dig in their heels to defend their privileges. In the pan-Afropean context, the communitarian accusation makes no sense. Were it to be formulated, it would be easy to shine a light

on the failings of the nations that have Afro-descendant populations. During the International Decade for People of African
Descent,[2] nothing of any significance was proposed by the United
Nations member states. Who then could reproach Afropeans for
taking care of their own affairs?

It is not for me to work out a pan-Afropean battle plan for
putting an end to Westernity and its corollaries. All I can do is suggest some avenues of thinking. Afropea will make its own decisions.
Nevertheless, it should be reminded of its status, first as the youngest
of Afro-descendant expressions, since the formulation of this ethnicity is recent, and second as the missing link between Afro-
descendants and sub-Saharans. Its European culture makes it close
to North America, with its own roots in Europe. Its proximities
with Africa make it close to Afro-descendants of the global South.
Thus it has a unique role to play. Afropea is a force of mediation
between Africa and Europe, which is how it first manifested itself.
Some of the European countries of which it is a citizen give it
broader significance, inasmuch as it embodies the experience both
of descendants of the colonized and of descendants of sub-Saharan
deportees. This is the case in France and Great Britain, for example,
countries that were enslaving and colonial powers.

In these environments, Afropea is even richer and the field of
its possibilities is considerable. When it engages in pan-Afropean
projects, it is with the ability to understand all viewpoints, which

---

2 The United Nations General Assembly proclaimed the decade 2015–2024 the
International Decade for People of African Descent, asking member states to set
up a variety of programmes in this framework.

increases its legitimacy. It brings a voice, an attitude and new aims to Europe. It ensures that the concerns and needs of the South are taken into account in the North. Originating from two worlds, which are still trapped in the shadows of their common history, Afropea can only live and act when it embodies the Ubuntu, the sub-Saharan concept that says, 'I am because we are.' All of us, humans whose existence has worth solely through our relationships. All of us, humans who have to be aware of the vulnerability at the core of our condition. Our illusions of power, our rejection of the other, our attachments to resentment speak of this. They say how very frail we are, and prompt, for this reason, to transfer this fragility to our fellow human beings. Toni Morrison said in an interview, 'If you can only be tall because someone is on their knees, then you have a serious problem.'[3] It is worth thinking about. The problem of domination resides in this neurotic need to crush others in order to feel superior to them. It is the sole motivation behind racism.

On a planet degraded by the spread of Westernity, the backlash will be—indeed already is—the obligation to get close and fraternize. If the decision is not made consciously, things will take a less peaceful turn. There may be no fraternity, but people will still be up against one another, in a concrete and intimate manner, until the end of time. By focusing on the experience and history of populations of sub-Saharan descent, Afropea, as the repository of that part

---

3 Toni Morrison, 'Novelist Toni Morrison Looks Back on Her Youth and Family and Presents Her Newest Book, *Jazz*', Interview with Charlie Rose (5 July 1993): https://charlierose.com/videos/18778 (last accessed on 24 May 2024).

of the silence imposed on so many peoples, rehabilitates the voices that were restrained and even denied. It is not simply a matter of mentioning their existence, but of hearing them and heeding their message. In the manner of the women healers who gathered from all continents to share their knowledge and speak to the world, calling themselves the Thirteen Indigenous Grandmothers,[4] Afropea aspires to deliver humanity from some of its woes. If there is no essence, no essential and unchanging human nature as such, if our behaviours result more from what inhabits our memories than from a fixed character, then there is nothing we cannot accomplish together. Provided we have the will, provided we recognize that we share the same humanity, and that no destination awaits some that does not also await others. By testifying to its hybridity—a word I employ here for lack of a better one to speak of the unity of sup-posedly opposite terms—Afropea reveals all the ethnicities of multiple belonging and all the other borderline identities that con-firm that alterity will always be present, that there will always be a need to make our way towards others. To meet others and meet ourselves in them.

---

4 See Carol Schaeffer, *Grandmothers Counsel of the World: Women Elders Offer Their Vision for Our Planet* (Boston, MA: Trumpeter, 2011).

A Utopia, for the Time Being

Afropea remains a utopia. It has great potential, but it is faced with powerful adversaries. Some readers of these pages may have been dumbfounded to hear someone dare advocate the end of Westernity. Living in an environment that is reluctant to acknowledge their presence, Afropeans are initially inclined to defensive strategies. Particularly in France, where racism is thriving more than ever and police brutalities serve as reminders of who is entitled to peacefully enjoy public space, Afropeans' first action is not to launch an attack on political formations and other institutions in order to work towards an end to Westernity. For them, it is first and foremost a matter of looking for the means to lead a relatively normal life and finding fulfilment if possible. And, because some injuries from history are still open wounds, it is also a matter of seeking reparation. France has said that the transoceanic deportations and colonial slavery were crimes against humanity, but it has not, even symbolically, designated a figure embodying the criminal, or pronounced a sanction. And the French government did not announce a single programme to implement in the framework of the International Decade for People of African Descent.

Not one, even though France is a member of the United
Nations, a part of what is called the international community, and
even though it includes many people of African descent among its
citizens. The NGOs lobbying to develop a series of measures and
activities during this ten-year period, which will come to an end
before anything is done, knocked on a great many doors, but in vain.
The fact is, in a country polluted by racism, terrified by the idea of
being invaded by hordes of sub-Saharans and reluctant to adopt a
spirit of responsibility for its colonial past, which it confuses with
an injunction to repent, merely indicating that people of African
descent exist is taken as a provocation. All the more if it is a question
of proposing a programme of events focusing on them or a series of
measures to include them in discussions of the country's identity.

Faced with this situation, many Afropeans are well beyond
the defensive strategies that had become second nature, the art of
dodging the sharp blades of a hostile society. They have no desire to
assimilate with colonizers, and are laying claim to a separation, at
least mentally. This speaks of a congestion of the mind, and even of
the soul. Some knots cannot be undone by those who are caught in
them. They would have needed a hand, and none was extended to
them in France. Just imagine what it is like to be at once a minority
and relegated to invisibility in a country where not all are treated
that way. Just imagine what it is like to have no representation of
oneself that is not caricatural and degrading. Just imagine what it
means to hear well-mannered gentlemen sitting around the table
in a fancy Parisian restaurant telling you that these people do not
exist, that what they have to say is not universal. What is systemic
racism if not this ability to exclude without even realizing it?

Setting its sights high, Afropea necessitates transcending legitimate grievances to the point of making its way to those who refuse
to see, to know, to share. Reaching out to them to propose a project
of transformation and elevation. It is not easy. Not as long as history glorifies the aggressors. Not as long as race-based seclusion
persists. The latter is of import here, for many Afro-descendants
have an attachment to race that stands in the way of the Afropean
project. This is because race determines the place of individuals in
society, because it is conflated with a part of history, and because
cultures and lifestyles are born of practices established to counter
its dehumanizing power. What are called Black cultures are those
that sprang out of the struggle not to sink, the constant negotiation
with the many faces of death, the victories against it, the reinvention of the self in places and circumstances where one was fated to
serve and to perish. The peoples that are called Black are repositories of that memory, and it is hard to see where to go if to arrive
there means leaving this baggage behind. It would be like betraying
one's ancestors, whose whole lives were a protest against violence,
who were cast out of the human family precisely because a racial
designation was applied to them. It would be like standing naked
before this world yet to be built, the world to come, when one feels
already so ill-equipped for self-realization in this one.

All this is understandable. There is no question of turning one's
back on a past that lives within, of disengaging from one's forebears,
of minimizing their suffering and the beauty that they managed
to create in spite of it. It is this *in spite of* that has to be made to
resonate. Those of whom we speak, our deported or colonized

sub-Saharan ancestors, had, above all, indissolubly embedded the consciousness of their humanity in their bodies. Being faithful to them involves restoring this to them and celebrating it. Such a positioning does not deny any of the torments of history; it merely moves them to a different place, by refusing to embrace victimhood, by turning pain into one's unique capital, the mainspring of one's identity. Consider Baby Suggs, the character in Toni Morrison's *Beloved.* Picture this impoverished woman, perceived as Black in the days of slavery, proclaiming herself a priestess and taking her community with her, teaching it self-love. What defines this woman and all those who were like her throughout history is not the colour of her skin, or even her sub-Saharan origin which is not a concern of hers. What defines her and strengthens the human community of which she is a part is the power of her spirit, her self-awareness, the meaning she gives to the freedom won, her capacity to build her world *in spite of* the other, the one who dominates.

It would be regrettable in the twenty-first century not to propose this vision of oneself to the oppressed of the world and to their oppressors. What Afropea seeks is not to abandon what constitutes a fundamental part of Afro-descendant experience but to embed it, to root it in universal consciousness. It is time to deracialize our perspectives. It would be better if the majority group, the privileged of the system, took the first step. They will not do so willingly, convinced as they are that they have more to lose than to gain from the transformation. The inclination would then be to stick to one's positions, to build a fortress in the silence and darkness that society offers, create the illusion of being solely with and for oneself. This is possible. Even feasible. The margins do not always bring misfortune, especially when they are abundantly peopled. But what would be the result?

Being unwilling to take the initiative on the pretext that it is up to others to do so, and because doing so would require recognizing an unbreakable bond with them, is the surest way to ensure the triumph of Westernity for centuries to come. This is in no one's interest. And those who do benefit from this could not care less about the ethical cost and live very comfortably with the nihilistic idea of *après moi, le déluge*. This is why minorities in France and elsewhere will be at the forefront of social and societal transformations. This is why they embody the ideals that others proclaim the better to betray them in their acts. Afropea is a go-between in the best sense of the term. It is the most noble thing it can represent. Making it into one more expression of Afro-descendant pain would divest it of its value. Regarding it as nothing but a Black identity on European soil would bring grist to the mill of cultural nationalists who see any category of Afro-descendance as representative of Africanity in exile. There will be no returning to an Africa that is not only not waiting for anyone but for which skin colour is an insufficient, indeed invalid, marker of belonging. It is by building on who one is and where one lives that one can work towards transforming the world. To do so, one must fully inhabit one's own abode.